ARTS & EATS

Recipes from Artists & Friends
of the Guilford Art Center

with Photographs by Joanne Schmaltz

Envisioned and organized by Maureen Belden and Lisa Wolkow.

Designed by Words by Jen, Branford, CT.

Printed in the United States of America.

Guilford Art Center
411 Church Street
Guilford, CT 06437

T: 203.453.5947
F: 203.453.6237
E: info@guilfordartcenter.org
Web: www.guilfordartcenter.org

ISBN: 978-0-615-19220-8

Guilford Art Center

The Guilford Art Center embraces the artistic interests of individuals and the well-being of the communities we serve. Our mission evolves from the idea that there is a gap between art and life. The gap is a dazzling space for artistic activity for all those with an interest in the arts. It is here that GAC lives and works with artists and art participants of all ages. We gather to dream, discover, practice, exhibit, teach, shop, and exchange ideas, while creating and preserving artistic traditions.

In the end, these activities become part of the fabric of our lives in ways both large and small and help shape the soul of the community. Involving individuals with art makes it possible for a community to create a richer, stronger, more culturally-diverse environment, and can move it from a good place to a thriving place to live.

Table of Contents

INTRODUCTION

Cooking Secrets

I've never met anyone who loves to cook who does not remember their first experiences in the kitchen and how they learned to get it right. My story is that I've been seriously at it since I was seven. When people seem surprised at this news, I explain my Mother did not enjoy cooking and my skills were developed in self-defense and a fondness for enjoying good food with my family. My progress was gradual, toast to bacon to fudge to spaghetti and finally, in seventh grade, homemade bread. This astounded my Mother, who had many bread failures in her past. We were both so happy as we talked about this new skill while we shared hunks of my latest, hot, buttered loaf. I said, "Mom, it is really easy. You just have to follow all of the directions."

Time went by. I learned to cook many more dishes, with a particular fondness for desserts. It was easy. I just followed all the directions sharing the results with my friends and family.

Then things changed and they changed over one recipe. I'd loved my Grandmother's cooking since I was a child, particularly her lemon pie. One day I complained to her I couldn't make a lemon pie as well as she could. She had me watch her make one and gave me the recipe. She said, "Just do everything the same way and it will be as delicious as mine." I still could not do it. She asked me to describe exactly how I made the pie. After listening she said, "You have to follow all the directions. If it's a lemon pie you have to use a yellow mixing bowl just like I did." Neither she nor the recipe said anything about a yellow bowl, but she had used one. So, I began using a yellow bowl, and frankly, while I managed to make more than a few that looked like hers, there was never as much pleasure eating mine as there was sharing hers.

You've guessed it: Two cooking secrets were revealed to me. First, some cooks have secrets they might not even know they have. Second, that hot buttered bread shared with someone I loved made the bread more delicious. Being with my Grandmother eating lemon pie made the pie better than any lemon pie I made and ate without her.

I'm really happy to be at the Guilford Art Center when it is releasing a new cookbook. It is a compelling combination of photographic images combined with amazing recipes. Each recipe was submitted by a cook someone knew as fantastic. I'm glad to add this one to my collection. I hope you are too. Remember. It is easy. Follow all the directions and share each wonderful dish with someone you enjoy. And, don't worry, no yellow bowls are required.

Jean Perkins
Executive Director
Guilford Art Center

APPETIZERS

Rosalie Rouillard

Baked Brie

1 medium Brie

1 package frozen puff pastry

1/2 cup brown sugar

1/2 cup toasted walnuts

1/2 cup dried cherries

1 egg mixed with 1 tbsp water for an egg wash

Thaw pastry according to directions. Cut Brie in half. Top bottom half with brown sugar, walnuts, cherries. Put on top half. Spread dough. Put Brie on top. Brush egg wash on edges. Top with other piece of dough. Seal edges well, cut extra or fold under Brie. Brush with egg wash. Bake at 400°F 15 to 20 minutes until golden brown.

Susan Guagliumi

This recipe makes enough dough to encrust two small wheels of Brie. Because it keeps so well in the freezer—and has to go from freezer to oven—it is a great make-ahead to keep on hand!

Brie en Croute

2 cups all-purpose flour

2 tsp baking powder

1 tsp salt

1/2 tsp dry mustard

2/3 cup shortening

1/2 cup boiling water

1 tbsp lemon juice

1 egg yolk for dough

1 egg yolk for wash

Garlic/onion jam, or other savory flavor (optional)

Combine dry ingredients in a large bowl. In a second bowl, combine shortening, boiling water, lemon juice, and 1 egg yolk. Stir into the flour mixture. When thoroughly mixed, divide pastry in half and wrap each in plastic wrap. Refrigerate until chilled, about 20 minutes. Roll out one piece of dough and use the top of the round Brie box to cut a circle of dough. Set aside. Re-roll dough to 11 to 12-inch circle. Place Brie, with outer coating intact, on the center of the dough and bring the pastry up over the cheese so it overlaps the top by about 1 inch. Beat remaining yolk with 1 tbsp water to make an egg wash and brush onto the edge of folded up pastry before pressing the reserved circle of dough on top. Brush the top with egg wash. Freeze the dough-wrapped cheese until solid; bake for 30 minutes in a 425°F oven. Let cool for 45 minutes before serving. Optional: Slit cheese horizontally and spread a savory jam or chutney between the layers before encrusting in the dough. Roll out scraps of dough and cut out leaf or other shapes to decorate the top of the wheel. Brush surface with egg wash first to make sure the decorations stick.

Feta Cheese Spread

3/4 cup feta cheese

1/4 cup goat (or cow) yogurt

1 tbsp dried dill weed

1 tbsp olive oil (more if desired)

1 tsp wine vinegar (white)

1/8 tsp ground chili pepper (optional)

Mix ingredients until smooth. Add more cheese or yogurt to create desired consistency.

Dolores

Marchese

This can be used on toasted, thinly cut Italian or French bread (drizzled with olive oil and heated in a 375°F oven). It is also good as a dip for vegetable crudités, especially cucumber slices, red and green peppers, celery and grape tomatoes.

Mary O'Connor

Fresh Mushroom Pate

1/2 lb mushrooms, chopped

2 tablespoons butter or margarine

1 (8-oz) package cream cheese, softened

1/4 teaspoon garlic salt

Sauté mushrooms in butter 5 to 10 minutes or until tender and liquid has evaporated. Place in blender or food processor; add remaining ingredients. Process until smooth. Chill, covered, at least 3 hours before serving. Garnish as desired. Serve on crackers or melba toasts. Makes 1 1/2 cups.

Guacamole

Raffaela Cipriano

4 tbsp finely chopped white onion, divided

1 1/2 tbsp coarsely chopped cilantro, divided

1 or 2 fresh serrano or jalapeno chilies, seeded, finely
chopped

1/4 tsp chopped garlic (optional)

2 large, soft-ripe avocados

1 medium, very ripe tomato or two plum tomatoes

1 to 2 tsp fresh lime juice

1/4 tsp salt

Corn tortilla chips

Chilies and cilantro sprig for garnish

Combine 2 tbsp onion, 1 tbsp cilantro, chilies and garlic
in large mortar. Grind with pestle until almost smooth.
Cut avocados lengthwise into halves, remove seed and
skin, place in a bowl. Add chili mixture and mash. Remove
seeds and liquid from tomatoes and cut into small chunks.
Add tomato, lime juice, salt and remaining 2 tbsp onion
and 1/2 tbsp cilantro to mixture and mix well. Makes
about 2 cups.

Homemade 'Boursin' Cheese

Margot Levy

1 clove garlic

3 tbsp butter at room temperature

1/2 tsp leaf marjoram, crumbled

1/8 tsp crumbled thyme

1/2 tsp coarsely ground pepper

1/8 tsp cayenne

2 8-oz packages cream cheese cut into slim pats

Turn food processor motor on, drop garlic down the tube and buzz for 2 seconds, scrape for 2 seconds. Add butter and seasonings, buzz for 5 seconds, scrape for 5 seconds. Add cream cheese, buzz for 10 seconds, scrape for 10 seconds. Firm in refrigerator and shape into loaf or log or serve in small bowl. Allow to season overnight in refrigerator. Let stand 30 minutes prior to serving. Alternatively, mince garlic, throw everything together and mix well…as long as butter and cream cheese are softened, it's easier than using processor!

Rosalie Rouillard

Hot Antipasto

2 cans artichoke hearts, quartered

2 cans sliced potatoes

1 can black olives, sliced

2 jars roasted peppers, drained and cut

1/2 cup grated parmesan cheese

1 1/2 cups flavored bread crumbs

1/4 cup olive oil (or to make low fat, olive oil spray)

Layer all ingredients in a 9 x 12 baking dish. Either drizzle olive oil over top or olive oil spray. Bake at 400°F for 30 minutes until brown.

Hot Artichoke and Crabmeat Dip

8 oz cream cheese, softened

1 cup mayonnaise

1 garlic clove, pressed

1 14-oz can of artichoke hearts in water, drained and chopped

8 oz imitation crabmeat, chopped

3/4 cup grated fresh parmesan cheese

1/2 cup thinly sliced green onions with tops (save a little less than half for end)

1/4 tsp grated lemon peel

2 dashes ground black pepper

1/4 cup chopped red bell pepper (mixed with leftover green onions)

Preheat oven to 350°F. Combine cream cheese, mayonnaise, and garlic. Mix well. Add artichokes, crabmeat, parmesan cheese, green onions, lemon zest and black pepper. Mix well. Spoon into a baking dish and bake for 25 to 30 minutes or until golden brown around edges. Top with red bell pepper and additional green onions.

Suzanne Hens-Kaplan

This is great with crackers, pita chips or bagel chips. It can also be microwaved.

Rosalie Rouillard

Hot Artichoke Dip

1 can artichokes, drained and cut into small pieces

1 cup mayonnaise (light or regular)

1 heaping cup Swiss cheese

1 clove garlic, finely chopped

Mix well, bake at 350°F for 20-25 minutes until it bubbles. Or microwave for 2 minutes, stir and microwave another minute. Serve with chips or pita.

Mary's Mustard Sauce

Mary Repetti

2 eggs

1/2 cup sugar

5 tbsp Colman's® dry mustard

1 tsp salt

Dash of white pepper

1/2 pint heavy cream

1/4 cup white vinegar

In top of double boiler beat 2 eggs with a wire whisk. Mix in sugar, mustard, salt and pepper and blend very well. Add cream. Cook, stirring occasionally, over boiling water until thickened, about 20-30 minutes, until mixture has a custard consistency. Remove from heat and while beating, add vinegar slowly. Cool and refrigerate…keeps for weeks! Makes 1 1/2 cups.

This sauce can be used in the traditional way as well as adding it to a basic vinaigrette, as a dip for veggies and pretzels, a grilling glaze for fish, pork, ham, and adding honey for a classic baked ham. It can easily be doubled.

Mousse de Foie de Volailles

1 lb duck, goose or chicken livers, cleaned and cut
  into 1/2 inch pieces

2 tbsp minced shallots

2 tbsp butter

1/3 cup Cognac or Madeira

1/2 cup melted butter

1/4 cup heavy cream

Pinch of thyme

1/2 tsp salt

Pepper to taste

Sauté shallots in the 2 tbsp of butter. Add livers and cook
for 3 to 5 minutes. Scrape into a blender's jar. Pour
Cognac or Madeira into skillet and reduce to 3 tbsp.
Scrape into blender's jar. Add to the blender all the rest
of the ingredients except for the melted butter. Blend at
top speed for a minute. Finally add the melted butter and
blend another few seconds. Force the mixture through
a fine sieve and adjust the taste. Serve with thin slices of
French bread.

**Lucienne
Coifman**

*This recipe was
passed to me from
my grandmother,
who was a chef
a long time ago.
It was translated
from the original
French to the best
of my ability. For
the 21st century,
we would use a
food processor and
finding duck or
goose livers may
be quite difficult.*

Carol Grave

*Best/easiest if
you have a food
processor.*

Olive Tapenade

1 bottle green olives

1 can black olives

Some sun-dried tomatoes packed in oil (optional)

Capers, to taste

Anchovies, if you want

Crumbled feta, if you want

Basically, just whir it all together to your liking and add
some olive oil to make a coarse paste. You can use the
ingredients you like and leave out the ones you don't. You
can use fancy or plain olives. Make a sandwich with some
cream cheese for a change of pace lunch.

Peppered Cheese

Margot Levy

8 oz Monterey Jack cheese, grated

8 oz cream cheese, at room temperature

1 tsp Herbes de Provence

1 tsp minced chives

1 tsp Worcestershire sauce

1 garlic clove, minced

Seasoned pepper

Combine all ingredients but seasoned pepper. Blend well. Shape into flattened ball. Roll ball in seasoned pepper on waxed paper till completely covered. Refrigerate. Make at least 1 day ahead to meld flavors.

Rosalie Rouillard

Southwestern Dip

I can refried beans

I can black beans

I can Mexican corn

I jar salsa

I cup shredded cheese (Mexican)

I can chopped green chilies (optional)

Mix all ingredients together, put in crock pot on low for 2 hours or microwave for 2 minutes, stir, microwave another minute.

Raffaela Cipriano

Takes 10 minutes
to prepare and a
few minutes
to cook.

Spicy Curried Mussels

2 shallots, finely chopped

1 1/4 tsp curry powder

1/4 tsp dried hot red pepper flakes, or to taste

1 tbsp unsalted butter

3 tbsp (+ or -) Sherry

1 1/2 to 2 tbsp of sweetened condensed coconut juice

2-3 lb cultivated mussels, scrubbed

3/4 cup half and half

2 tbsp chopped fresh cilantro

Accompaniment: crusty bread

Cook shallots, curry powder, and red pepper flakes in butter in a 5- to 6-quart heavy pot over moderate heat, stirring, until shallots are softened, about 4 minutes. Add Sherry and coconut juice. Simmer, stirring, 1 minute. Add mussels. Cook, covered, over moderately high heat 4 to 6 minutes, checking periodically after 4 minutes and transferring mussels as opened to a bowl. Discard any unopened mussels after 6 minutes. Add half and half to pot and bring to a boil. Add cilantro and salt to taste, then pour over mussels and toss lightly. Serves 2 as a main dish, serves many for an appetizer.

Stromboli

Kathy Morrell

2 packages crescent rolls

1/3 lb domestic ham, thin sliced

1/3 lb salami, thin sliced

1/3 lb slicing pepperoni, sliced thin

1/3 lb Provolone cheese

1/3 lb Swiss cheese

6 tbsp Parmesan cheese

1 jar roasted red peppers, drained

6 eggs

Roll out one package of crescent rolls in bottom of a 13 x 9 baking pan. Layer ham, Swiss, salami, Provolone, and slicing pepperoni. Add second layer in same order. Top with roasted peppers. Mix 4 eggs and 4 tbsp of Parmesan cheese. Pour over top of meat. Top with second package of crescent rolls. Mix 2 eggs and 2 tbsp Parmesan cheese and pour over rolls. Bake at 400°F covered with foil for 30 minutes. Bake an additional 30 minutes uncovered. Best when served warm.

Rosalie Rouillard

Stuffed Mushrooms

1 lb fresh large mushrooms

2 garlic cloves, minced

1 medium onion, chopped fine

1 tbsp butter

1 tsp olive oil

1/4 cup sherry

1 cup flavored bread crumbs

Separate mushroom caps from stems, chop stems. Sauté garlic, onions and stems in oil and butter for 3-5 minutes. Add sherry and cook 2-3 minutes. Add bread crumbs and stir until moist. Stuff caps with stuffing mixture. Put in a baking pan with water on the bottom. Bake at 350°F for 30 minutes.

Susan's Salsa

Sabine Harris

1 pint cherry tomatoes

1 small can of corn

1/2 red pepper

1 green pepper

1/2 can of black beans

1/2 onion

1/2 cup cilantro

1 jalapeno pepper

1 tsp grated ginger

1 large clove garlic

Cut everything into very small pieces and mix. Refrigerate for at least two hours. Serve with some good chips.

Tzatziki

Malcolm Davis

2 cucumbers (peeled) or 1 long English cucumber
(don't peel if organic)

4 cups plain yogurt (non fat or low fat)

1 tbsp, or less, sea salt or kosher salt

1 tbsp of dill weed (dry or fresh)

1 tbsp fresh lemon juice

1 tbsp rice vinegar

2 tbsp olive oil

1/4 teaspoon ground black pepper

4 to 6 cloves or more of garlic, minced or crushed

1 cup sour cream (optional)

Cilantro and/or mint (optional)

Strain yogurt for several hours to separate the whey and
thicken; (a large coffee filter works). Chop cucumbers and
put in colander; sprinkle with salt to get out the water;
let set for several hours. Squeeze water from chopped
cucumbers and mix with strained yogurt. Add all the other
ingredients and mix well. Chill.

Bevi Bullwinkel

This crabmeat dip came from my late brother who worked in Maryland one summer. It can be made one day in advance and refrigerated (covered).

Walt's Crabmeat Dip

1/2 cup chili sauce

1/2 cup mayonnaise

1 clove garlic, finely chopped

1/2 tsp dry mustard

1 tbsp horseradish

1 tsp Tabasco®

1/2 tsp salt

2 finely chopped hard cooked eggs

1 cup fresh flaked crabmeat (canned or frozen can be substituted)

Mix all ingredients together, saving the crabmeat and eggs for last. Be sure to drain the crabmeat before adding. Serve with Melba toast or crackers of your choice.

Watermelon Salsa

DeeDee Hakun

1/2 seedless watermelon

1 bunch chopped scallion

1 diced red bell pepper

1 cup chopped cilantro

3 limes or lemons

1 tbsp chile or finely chopped jalapeno pepper

Combine scallion, red bell pepper, cilantro, lime or lemon juice, chiles and a pinch of salt. Add watermelon. Let chill and serve. Serves 6.

Wrapped Dates

**Leslie Ann
Powers**

*These will
disappear in
minutes!*

1 package pitted dates (check for missed pits)

1 lb low salt bacon slices

1 jar Open Pit® barbecue sauce (original)

Cut bacon into 1/3 lengths. Place a paper towel on a
plate. Layer bacon pieces on the paper towel, then top
with another paper towel. It usually takes about 4 layers of
bacon and towel per batch. Place in microwave oven for
3 minutes (on high) at a time until bacon is partly cooked.
Keep checking until it's lightly brown. Too cooked will
break when wrapped. Using toothpicks, wrap each date
with one piece of bacon, and place them on a cooling
rack. (This can be done ahead and refrigerated.)

Just before serving, place the rack on a cookie sheet and
brush each date with the barbecue sauce. Bake for 10
minutes in a 300°F oven. Check to make sure the bacon
is cooked. Serves 6 to 8.

SOUPS

Robin L.
Bergman

*This is one of my
very favorite and
simple recipes.
It's good any time
of year and is
served at room
temperature.
Although simple
to make and
healthy, it is
elegant as well.*

Avgolemono Soup with Carrots

1/2 lb carrots, grated coarse

5 cups chicken broth

3 large eggs

5 tbsp fresh lemon juice

1 tbsp snipped fresh dill (or to taste)

White pepper (to taste)

Snipped sprigs of fresh dill for garnish

In a stainless steel or enamel saucepan combine the carrots and the broth. Bring to a boil, and simmer the mixture, covered, for 5 minutes, or until the carrots are just tender. In a bowl with an electric mixer* beat the eggs until they are thick and cream colored and add the lemon juice in a very slow stream, beating. Add 1 cup of the hot broth in a very slow stream, still beating. Add the egg mixture to the carrot mixture in a slow stream, stirring. Cook the soup over moderately low heat, stirring, until it is thickened slightly and a thermometer registers 180°F, but do not let it boil (it should just start to coat the back of the spoon). Transfer the soup to a large serving bowl, stir in the snipped dill, white pepper and salt to taste and let the soup cool. Chill the soup, covered, for at least 3 hours or overnight so the flavors meld. Ladle the soup into chilled bowls and garnish with the dill sprigs. Makes about 6 cups/6 servings.

I use a food processor fitted with the steel blade and keep the motor running while I slowly add the lemon juice from the tube, and then the hot broth.

Beef Barley Soup

Kathy Morrell

6 slices bacon

1 1/2 pounds stew beef

4 stalks celery, sliced

4 to 6 carrots, sliced thick

Mushrooms - sliced

1/2 red pepper - sliced and cubed

1/2 cup pearl barley- rinsed and drained

6 cans (14-oz) beef broth

1 tsp fresh thyme

1 bay leaf

1 large onion chopped

1 tsp basil

1 tsp oregano

1 garlic clove - chopped

1 tsp balsamic vinegar

1 cup corn

1 cup broccoli

1/8 tsp black pepper

Brown bacon in a large stock pot. Remove bacon. Add stew beef into bacon fat, simmer until browned. Remove beef, add carrots, celery, onion, red pepper, and barley. Cook on medium-low heat 10 to 15 minutes until tender. Add mushrooms and spices. Cook 5 minutes. Return stew beef and juices to pot, add beef broth and balsamic vinegar. Heat to a boil, then reduce heat to low. Simmer uncovered until the beef is fork tender (approx. 2 hours). Add corn, broccoli, and black pepper. Simmer 10 to 15 minutes until the broccoli is tender.

Beef Tomato Broth

Helen H.
Fletcher

2 1/2 cups beef broth

1 1/4 cups tomato juice

1 small onion stuck with 6 cloves

3 tbsp sugar

1/2 tsp Worcestershire sauce

1/4 tsp Tabasco® sauce

1/8 tsp baking soda

Heat ingredients over moderate heat for 5 minutes.
Discard onion. Ladle soup into bowls, garnish with thin
slice of orange. Serves 4.

Laurie Semke

*Great served with
sour cream and/
or chopped green
onions. A garnish
of crisp chips is
good, too.*

Black Bean Soup

I cup black beans, soaked

3 15-oz cans chicken broth

I tbsp olive oil

I onion

I clove garlic

1/4 cup diced celery

1/2 cup diced carrots

I tsp ground cumin

1/4 tsp black pepper

1/4 tsp salt (if needed)

Wash and sort beans. Cover with cold water and soak
overnight; or to quick soak, boil beans for 2 minutes, turn
off the heat and let stand I hour. Drain the beans and add
broth. Bring beans to a boil, then reduce heat and simmer
for 2 to 3 hours or until beans are cooked. In a skillet,
sauté onion and garlic in the oil until transparent. Add
the celery and carrots and cook for 5 minutes. Add the
vegetables to the beans, then season with cumin, pepper
and salt, and simmer another 30 minutes. Puree the soup
in a blender or food processor and serve hot.

Lentil Soup

Rosalie Rouillard

1 lb lentils

1 large onion, chopped

1 cup celery, chopped

1 cup carrots, chopped

3 to 4 garlic cloves, minced

1/4 cup fresh parsley

4 cups water

4 bouillon cubes

1 can crushed tomatoes

Wash and rinse lentils and place in a soup pot with water. Simmer for one hour. Add remaining ingredients and simmer for another hour.

Judy Siccama

This is my mom's recipe—delicious! Every time I serve it, people ask for the recipe!

Leota's Cream of Carrot Soup

4 tbsp butter

6 carrots sliced

2 medium potatoes peeled and sliced

1 small onion

1 cup chicken broth

1/2 tsp pepper

1/2 tsp salt

1 cup milk (light if calorie counting)

Dash paprika

Dash nutmeg

Melt butter in pan, add broth, salt, pepper, and vegetables. Cook until tender. Cool, puree in blender or food processor. Return to pan, add milk, nutmeg, and paprika. (For added flavor I braise the vegetables in an ironstone pan for 30 minutes to an hour, until the vegetables have changed in color, before adding the broth. Then proceed as above. Love the taste.)

David Frank

A flavorful soup, made mostly from ingredients already on the kitchen shelf. Serve with fresh, crusty bread for a hearty meal. This recipe comes from Yankee Magazine New England Church Supper Cookbook. *It was given to me by a customer for whom I made soup bowls. It is one of my favorites.*

Main Dish Minestrone

1 tbsp olive oil

1/2 lb sweet or hot sausage, crumbled

1 large onion, chopped

1 garlic clove, minced

1/2 cup chopped celery

1/2 cup chopped carrot

1/2 cup chopped green bell pepper

1 16-oz can whole tomatoes

4 cups chicken stock or broth

2 cups shredded cabbage

2 tbsp chopped fresh parsley

1/2 tsp dried basil

1 bay leaf

Pinch dried thyme

1/2 cup uncooked elbow macaroni

1 cup cooked kidney beans

Freshly grated Parmesan cheese (optional)

In a large saucepan or stockpot, heat the oil. Add the sausage and cook until browned. Drain off all but 1 teaspoon of the fat. Add the onions, garlic, celery, carrot, and green pepper and sauté until vegetables are soft, about 5 minutes. Add the tomatoes with their liquid, chicken stock, cabbage, and herbs. Bring to a boil, cover, and simmer for 30 minutes. Add the macaroni and beans and cook until macaroni is tender, about 30 minutes. Remove bay leaf before serving. Sprinkle each serving with Parmesan cheese, if desired.

Pasta Fagioli

Rosaria I. Juska

2 cans dark red kidney beans, drained

1 whole red bell pepper, chopped

1 large onion, chopped

1/2 cup olive oil

1/2 lb spaghettini broken up (approx. in 1 inch in length)

2 tbsp salt (optional)

Crushed red pepper

Grated Parmesan cheese

In a 3-quart saucepan, pour drained red kidney beans. Add chopped red bell pepper, onion, and olive oil. Stir and cook on medium-low heat, stirring occasionally. In a 4-quart stock pot, bring water to a boil, add pasta and salt. Stir and do not overcook pasta. Once pasta is cooked, you want to leave some of the broth (water) with the pasta. So, drain the pasta but not fully. Place pasta in a serving bowl and add bean mixture. Mix together well. Serve with grated parmesan cheese and crushed red pepper sprinkled on top.

Lady McCrady

*This will make
a cool lunch for
three or four days.
It makes you very
thin, very tan,
and very happy
every day. Serve
in a wide-mouth
French coffee cup
or small bowl.
Polka dot ones are
nice, as is a huge
silver spoon.*

Riviera Club Gazpacho

1 onion

1 green pepper

1 cucumber (preferably English)

Tomato juice

2 tbsp cold press olive oil

2 tbsp cider vinegar

Salt and pepper to taste

1 clove of garlic, chopped (optional)

In a food chopper, chop the onion, green pepper and cucumber. Fill a big jar for the refrigerator with tomato juice, olive oil, cider vinegar, salt and pepper. Add the vegetables. Serve with a few fresh mint leaves, if desired, or stir with a celery stalk, or add a dollop of sour cream or good organic yogurt.

Robin L.
Bergman

Robin's Gazpacho

3 bell peppers (any colors, mixed is fine), chopped

1 large red onion, chopped medium fine

4 to 5 scallions, chopped

1 small bunch cilantro, chopped

1 long English cucumber, or 2 regular cucumbers, peeled, cut in 1/2 lengthwise and seeds scooped out, chopped

1 pint grape or cherry tomatoes, cut in 1/2 or 1/4

5 large garlic cloves, peeled and chopped

3 large radishes, peeled and chopped

2 jalapeno chiles, seeded and chopped (use gloves to handle)

3 to 4 cups of low-salt tomato or vegetable juice.

2 tbsp olive oil

3 to 5 tbsp balsamic vinegar (to taste, can add 3 now and adjust later)

1/4 tsp freshly ground black pepper

1/4 - 1/2 tsp sea salt

3 to 4 drops Tabasco® Sauce, to taste

Vietnamese hot chili sauce - adds extra fire but is not as sharp (optional)

Fresh croutons, for serving

Mix the vegetables and put 1/2 to 3/4 of the mixture into a food processor or blender (depending on how chunky you want your gazpacho). Add tomato or vegetable juice, olive oil, balsamic vinegar, black pepper, sea salt, Tabasco® Sauce, and Vietnamese hot chili sauce, if using. Puree, but not too finely. Add together with remaining chopped vegetables. Adjust seasonings to taste. Chill. Serves 8 to 12.

Seafood Gazpacho

Patty Langdon

2 cups fresh bread crumbs

3 minced garlic cloves

1 cucumber, peeled, seeded and diced

2 sweet red peppers, peeled, seeded and diced

3 jalapeno peppers, peeled, seeded and diced, or red
    pepper flakes, to taste

1 medium onion, chopped

5 ripe tomatoes, seeded and chopped

5 cups tomato juice

Juice of 4 limes

1/2 cup olive oil

1 tbsp (or less) cumin

Salt and pepper, to taste

1 lb lump crab meat

1 ripe avocado, peeled and diced

Combine bread crumbs and garlic cloves. Combine
cucumber, red peppers, jalapeno peppers, onion, and
tomatoes. Add tomato juice and lime juice. Add the bread
crumb mixture to the tomato mixture and then stir in
1/2 cup olive oil. Puree half the soup in a food processor
or blender, then add the other half, not pureed, back in.
Season with cumin, salt and pepper, and refrigerate. Just
before serving, add crab meat and avocado.

Swiss Chard and Great Northern Bean Soup
SERVED OVER THAI RED RICE

Barbara
Hanselman

This is a fast but hearty vegetarian soup – great for a winter's meal!

6 to 10 large cloves organic garlic, minced

2 tbsp cold-pressed organic olive oil

2 tsp dried oregano*

1 tbsp fresh minced basil*

1 to 2 tsp rosemary, smashed in a mortar & pestle*

1/2 tsp dried red pepper flakes (or to taste)*

1 large bunch (8 to 12 large leaves) of green or rainbow Swiss chard, washed, de-veined and chopped

3 15-oz cans Westbrae Natural® Organic Great Northern beans (do not drain, use liquid in the soup); drain one can and mash the beans from that can with a fork on a large plate

1 cup vegetable broth

1 tbsp grated sheep's milk such as Locatelli® (optional)

1 tbsp crumbled Parlick sheep's milk cheese (optional, but rich in flavor)

Salt to taste

2 cups Thai red rice, cooked as per package directions (available at Asian markets).

Sauté garlic in 1 tbsp of olive oil till tender. Add spices, chard and remaining olive oil. Stir to coat the chard and cook about 3 minutes until wilted. Add remaining ingredients and cover. Cook over very low heat for about 8 to 10 minutes. Serve over red rice garnished with crumbled Parlick sheep's milk cheese and fresh basil. *Use spices in amounts which you favor. If you like one spice more than the other, use them accordingly.*

SALADS

Lady McCrady

Art Matters Red, Yellow, Green and Purple Picnic Salad

SALAD:

4 cups cooked rice

1/3 cup green pepper and red pepper

1/4 cup red onion, chopped

1/4 cup fresh parsley, chopped

DRESSING:

1 cup olive oil

2/3 cup white wine vinegar

2 tbsp lemon juice

1 1/2 tbsp curry

1 clove garlic

2 tbsp sugar

Combine ingredients for dressing and toss with rice and vegetables.

Bean Salad

Margot Levy

SALAD:

1 can kidney beans

1 can green beans

1 can waxed beans

1 can small green lima beans

1 can chick peas/garbanzo beans

1/2 cup chopped onion

1/2 cup chopped green pepper

1 cup diced celery

DRESSING:

1 tsp salt

1/2 tsp ground black pepper

3/4 cup sugar

1/2 cup vinegar

1/2 cup vegetable oil

Stir dressing until sugar melts. Pour over vegetables and mix. Cover and refrigerate for 24 hours, stirring occasionally.

Chicken Pecan Salad

Raffaela Cipriano

*This recipe can be
easily multiplied.*

1 cup cubed cooked white chicken meat

2 tsp chopped fresh tarragon

1/4 cup mayonnaise

1/4 cup sour cream

1/4 cup finely diced celery

1/4 cup chopped pecans

Salt and fresh ground pepper to taste

1/2 cup red seedless grapes, sliced in half

Red and green peppers, apples, pears, or any other
  vegetable or fruit, cut in small cubes, as desired
  (optional)

Combine all ingredients in a large mixing bowl. Spoon
on top of lettuce cups, cucumber slices, or serve for
sandwiches. Makes 1 1/2 cups.

Joan Downey

Easy Crunchy Salad

Bed of romaine lettuce

Package of "broccoli slaw"

1 onion, red or sweet, sliced

1 can black olives

Nuts of your choice

Blue Cheese dressing, or a mixture of Light Italian and
   Blue Cheese

Assemble all ingredients in order and toss.

Feta Bulghur Salad

Susan Kukle

1/2 cup dry coarse ground bulghur grain

1 small carrot, chopped

3 sprigs parsley, chopped

1/4 cup red onion, chopped

1/4 cup chopped pepper

1/2 stalk celery, chopped

1/2 cup feta cheese, crumbled

1/4 cup vinaigrette

1/2 cup cucumber, chopped

2 tomatoes, seeded and chopped

Rinse dry bulghur in cold water. Pour 1 cup boiling water to allow bulghur to absorb for about 1/2 hour. Drain any water. Add remaining ingredients.

This recipe can also be made with lentils instead of bulghur. Simmer 1 cup lentils in water to cover for 10 minutes. Drain and cool. Add remaining ingredients, tossing to mix well.

Gretchen
Halpert

Fresh Cabbage, Fennel and Pineapple Salad

2 cups fresh green cabbage, chopped

1 cup fresh fennel, chopped

1/2 cup fresh pineapple

Shavings of purple cabbage, for color (optional)

Combine all ingredients. Sprinkle with fennel seeds and top with a light balsamic vinaigrette.

**Debbie
Staub Luft**

*This recipe is
adapted from* Fine
Cooking,
July 2005.

Green Bean Salad with Corn, Cherry Tomatoes and Basil

3 cups blanched corn kernels

1 lb green beans

1 pint cherry tomatoes

1 bunch scallions, green and white roughly chopped

1 cup basil, roughly chopped

3 cloves garlic

1/8 cup wine vinegar

1/3 cup olive oil

Juice of 1 lemon

Salt and pepper to taste

Boil green beans about 3 minutes. Cool immediately. Chill beans and blanched corn kernels. Assemble vinaigrette: mash garlic cloves in a bowl, add lemon juice, red wine vinegar, olive oil and salt and pepper. Toss green beans, corn, tomatoes, scallions and basil with vinaigrette. Serve immediately.

Mexican Salad

Ann Person

1 lb lean ground beef, ground turkey or 3 cups shredded
 cooked chicken

1 package taco mix

1 15-oz can kidney beans, drained

1 cup shredded cheddar cheese

2 cups tortilla chips broken into small pieces

2 cups shredded lettuce

Brown meat mixture and drain. Add beans and taco
mix and simmer. Just prior to serving add remaining
ingredients. Top with avocado, tomato wedges, ripe olives
or sour cream if desired.

Mom's "Cuc" Salad

Kathleen
DePalma

1 cucumber

1/2 medium onion

1/2 cup white vinegar

1/2 cup water

1 1/2 tbsp sugar

1/4 tsp salt

Dash pepper

Pull tines of fork on length of cucumber. Slice both onion and cucumber thinly. Combine remaining ingredients and pour over vegetables. Marinate at least one hour.

Genie Copp

Pottery Salad, or Last Class Salad

DRESSING:

1/3 cup vinegar

2/3 cup olive oil

1/2 to 1 tsp coarse mustard

1/2 to1 tsp chopped garlic

Shake dressing ingredients and pour over a mix of lettuce, spinach, and spring greens. Sprinkle with sunflower seeds, Craisins®, feta cheese and chopped olives.

Riviera Club Salade de Pomme de Terre

Lady McCrady

Combine boiled new potatoes, mayonnaise, pepper, and small amount of red onion. Add one tin of anchovies in oil, finely chopped. Add a handful of fresh tarragon, crushed.

The first Riviera Club I ever knew was the one in Indianapolis. It had 5 massive pools with every kind of slide and platform into it, a child's dream of perfect summer. They made it affordable for everyone to join, a democratic "club" that was still way chic. Miles Davis played at the one that was further west, and we named our studio "Villa Riviera." This "potato salad" never ceases to amaze. Take it along when you ply the Connecticut River from Essex in an antique river boat like Nifty.

Tortellini Salad

Kathy Morrell

2 packages cheese tortellini

2 cups blanched broccoli

1 cup red pepper, cut into thin strips and blanched

Zucchini and carrots, cut into small pieces and blanched

1 small can sliced black olives, drained

1 cup Parmesan cheese

1 package Good Seasons® Italian Dressing - made with
   balsamic vinegar and olive oil

Cook tortellini according to directions—do not
overcook—and drain. Add blanched vegetables and black
olives. Mix Good Seasons®, balsamic and olive oil as
directed. Add Parmesan cheese. Pour over tortellini and
vegetables while warm. Refrigerate at least 3 hours before
serving.

BREADS & BREAKFAST

Diane Petra

*I learned this
recipe in a cooking
class with Betty
Ann Donegan.*

Buttery Pear Muffins

2 cups fresh pears, Bartlett or Comice, peeled and
    chopped

3/4 cup sugar

1/2 cup butter, melted and cooled

2 extra large eggs

1 tsp vanilla

1 1/2 cups Gold Medal® flour

1 tsp baking powder

1 tsp baking soda

1/2 tsp salt

3/4 cup chopped pecans or other nuts

Preheat oven to 350°F. Grease or line 12 muffin cups. In
a large bowl, toss chopped pears with the sugar and set
aside. In another bowl blend eggs with melted butter and
vanilla and set aside. In a third bowl stir together flour,
baking powder, baking soda, and salt. Stir in chopped nuts.
Stir egg mixture into pear mixture. Stir dry ingredients
into pear mixture, just until combined. Spoon batter into
muffin cups and bake 20 minutes or until muffins test clean
in center.

Easter Bread

Lil Levine

6 cups flour

4 eggs

2 packages yeast

1/2 cup milk

1 stick unsalted butter melted

1/4 warm water

1 cup sugar

Combine water and 2 tbsp of sugar with yeast and let rise. When it has risen, combine all other ingredients, adding the flour a little at a time. Knead your dough and then place in a large bowl to rise for 3 hours. After 3 hours knead and then divide the dough into 4 loaves. Place the loaves on a greased cookie sheet and let rise for 1 hour. Before putting the dough into the oven, brush with an egg yolk glaze. Bake at 350°F for 40 minutes. Makes 4 loaves.

English Muffin Bread

Judy Siccama

*This recipe was
given to me by
McKenzie Barrett
of East Haven,
Connecticut.*

1 tbsp yeast (or 1 packet)

1 tbsp sugar

1/2 cup warm (109°F) water

2 1/2 cups flour

1 tsp salt

1 cup milk (any kind)

1 tbsp warm water

1/4 tsp of baking soda

Place yeast, sugar, and water in a small bowl. Stir to mix and let proof. In a large bowl mix the flour and salt. Warm the milk to 109°F on the stove. Add the risen yeast to the warm milk. Add this mixture to the flour and salt. Stir to mix completely. The dough will be soft and very sticky. Cover with plastic wrap and put in a warm place to double in size. Mix the water and baking soda until the soda is melted. Punch down the dough after it has risen. In the bowl add the combined 1 tablespoon of warm water with 1/4 teaspoon of baking soda. Stir well or you will get brown streaks in the finished loaf.

Butter and flour a bread pan and place the dough in it to let it rise to double. While the dough is rising preheat the oven to 350°F for a metal pan or 325°F for a glass one. Bake 45 to 50 minutes or until it is brown and bread sounds hollow when rapped in the center. Remove from pan and let cool on a wire rack.

David and
Gina Frank

French Bread

1/2 tsp sugar

1 1/4 cups lukewarm water

1 package dry yeast

About 2 3/4 cups bread flour or all-purpose flour

1 1/2 tsp kosher salt

Cornmeal for sprinkling

In a large mixing bowl, stir the sugar into the water. Add the yeast, and stir to dissolve. Let stand until foamy, 3 to 5 minutes. Beat in 1 cup of the flour and the salt. Gradually add the remaining 1 3/4 cups flour, stirring after each addition. Transfer the dough to a lightly floured surface and knead until smooth and elastic. Use additional flour, if necessary, to prevent the dough from sticking. Put the dough in a lightly buttered medium bowl. Grease the surface with butter, cover with a damp cloth (warm to hot water), and set aside in a warm place to rise for about 1 hour, or until almost doubled. At least 15 minutes before you bake, preheat the oven to 400°F. Sprinkle a baking sheet with the cornmeal and set aside. Fill a large cast-iron skillet halfway with water and place on the bottom of the oven. Punch down the dough and divide it in half. With a rolling pin or your hands, roll each piece into a rectangle and shape about 1/2 inch thick. Using your hands, roll the rectangles into logs, pinching the ends of the logs to seal. Transfer to the baking sheet and brush lightly with water. I add sea salt to the top of the bread.

Bake for 25 to 30 minutes, or until the bread makes a hollow sound when tapped, brushing with water several times as the bread cooks. Cool completely on a wire rack before slicing. Makes 2 loaves.

French Toast Soufflé

Mary Beeman

A firm white bread, or even better, cinnamon raisin bread, produces the best texture in this make-ahead breakfast casserole.

10 cups 1-inch cubed sturdy white bread, such as
  Pepperidge Farm® Hearty White (about 16 1-oz slices)
Cooking spray
1 8-oz block 1/3-less-fat cream cheese, or regular,
  softened
8 large eggs
1 1/2 cups 2% reduced-fat milk
2/3 cup half-and-half
1/2 cup maple syrup
1/2 tsp vanilla extract
2 tbsp powdered sugar
3/4 cup maple syrup

Place bread cubes in a 9"x13" baking dish coated with cooking spray. Beat cream cheese at medium speed of mixer until smooth. Add eggs, one at a time, mixing well after each addition. Add milk, half-and-half, 1/2 cup maple syrup, and vanilla, and mix until smooth. Pour cream cheese mixture over top of bread; cover and refrigerate overnight. Preheat over to 375°F. Remove bread mixture from refrigerator; let stand for 30 minutes. Bake for 50 minutes or until set. Sprinkle the soufflé with powdered sugar, and serve with maple syrup. Serves 12 (or 6 teenage boys).

David Alban

*This recipe is from
my family. It is a
great long weekend
thing. Some of the
timing over night
to rise is because
of the old cold
Iowa farmhouses
we lived in. Those
times can be sped
up some in the
event of central
heating! When
I was a kid we
used to prop my
Swedish great
grandmother up
in the kitchen and
she directed.*

Limpa Christmas Bread

3 lbs rye-graham flour

1/2 gallon molasses

1 pint dark corn syrup

2 tbsp salt

2 quarts water

2 tbsp each of caraway, fennel, celery seeds, and anise

1 box candied orange peel, cut fine

3 cakes Fleishman's® yeast

6 cups warm water

3 quarts white flour

Scald rye-graham flour and add other ingredients, through
candied orange peel, and 1 quart white flour. Let stand
over night. In the morning add 3 cakes of Fleishman's®
yeast, 6 cups warm water and 2 quarts white flour. Stir
several times that day and in the evening work it up stiff
with as much flour as needed. Grease the top and set
in a warm place overnight. Mold into oblong flat loaves
and put on a large cookie sheet. Let rise for an hour and
prick with fork. Then bake in a medium hot oven (375°F).
Brush the top with sugar syrup. This makes 20 loaves
so it can be cut in half, (a good idea for the first batch
especially.) Store in a stone jar with several apples to keep
moist.

Mary Lou Fiore

*This recipe makes
2 loaves and we
use coffee cans for
molds covered with
double thickness of
wax paper.*

Mom's Brown Bread

2 cups sour milk

3/4 cup molasses

1 cup bran

1 cup cornmeal

1 cup raisins

2 tsp baking soda

2 tbsp sugar

1 1/2 tsp salt

1 tsp cinnamon

Combine sour milk, molasses, and bran. Let stand about
10 minutes or until most of the liquid is absorbed by the
bran. Combine dry ingredients and raisins; fold into the
bran mixture and stir just enough to moisten the dry
ingredients. Do not beat. Fill greased molds 2/3 full and
cover with greased covers made of parchment paper or
wax paper. Place into a large pan with water up to half of
mold and steam about 3 hours. Uncover and bake in a
slow oven, 250°F for 10 minutes, just until tops are dry.

Oatmeal Bran Muffin Mix

Carol Grave

*This recipe can be
halved; but the
batter keeps in
refrigerator for 6
weeks, so you can
have fresh baked
muffins every day!*

2 cups boiling water

2 cups 100% bran (unprocessed, not the cereal)

1 cup canola or other oil

3 cups sugar: white, brown or mixed (try a little less if
   you want)

4 eggs

1 quart buttermilk

5 cups flour: white, whole wheat or mixed; use a bit less
   flour if using all whole wheat

1 tsp salt

5 tsp baking soda

4 cups rolled oats (or use some rolled oats and some
   bran buds)

Optional just prior to baking: raisins, dried cranberries,
   chopped dried dates, nuts, flax seed or other crunchies,
   to taste

Pour boiling water over the bran and set aside to cool
to room temperature. Mix oil and sugars. Add eggs,
buttermilk, flour, salt, and soda. Mix well. Add oats and
the bran mixture. Fill well-oiled or paper lined muffin tins
3/4 full and bake at 375°F for 15 to 20 minutes; for batter
just out of fridge, bake 20-35 minutes. Remember to add
nuts and dried fruits just prior to baking. Be creative.

Ostkaka

4 quarts fresh whole milk, lukewarm

1 1/2 cups cream

3/4 cup flour

1/2 rennet tablet

1/2 cup cold water

3 eggs, beaten

3/4 cup sugar

1/2 tsp almond extract

1/2 tsp salt

Heat milk. Make thin paste of flour with part of milk. Stir into milk. Soak rennet tablet in water for 3 minutes. Add to milk. Stir well, and let stand 40 minutes. Stir curds, put into cheesecloth and drain off whey. Combine eggs, sugar, salt, cream, and extract. Combine mixtures. Turn into a 1 1/2-quart greased baking dish. Bake in a moderately hot oven (400°F) for 20 minutes. Reduce oven to 350°F for 45 minutes. Cool and serve with fresh strawberries.

David Alban

This is like a Swedish cheesecake, or custard. It is always set out at midsummer with strawberries. It is best with milk right outta the cow!

Robert Parrott

Pane al Pomodoro
TOMATO BREAD

1 clove garlic

2 tbsp finely chopped onion

1 tbsp oil from sun-dried tomatoes

2 1/2 tsp (1 package) active dry yeast or 1 small cake (18 grams) fresh yeast

1/4 cup warm water

1 cup water, room temperature

1/3 to 1/2 cup coarsely chopped sun-dried tomatoes, packed in oil

3 3/4 cups unbleached all-purpose flour

2 tsp salt

1 egg white beaten

Lightly sauté garlic and onion in oil; let cool to room temperature. Stir yeast into the warm water in a large mixing bowl; let stand until creamy, about 10 minutes. Stir 1 cup water, the garlic and onion with the oil; then stir in the tomatoes. Mix the flour and salt; stir 1 cup at a time into the yeast mixture. Knead on a lightly floured surface, sprinkling in 2 to 3 tbsp additional flour as needed, until dough is soft, velvety and slightly moist, 8 to 10 minutes. Place in a lightly oiled bowl, cover with plastic wrap, and let rise until doubled, about 1 hour. Punch the dough down on a lightly floured surface and knead briefly. Shape into a ball. Place on a lightly oiled baking sheet. Cover with a towel and let rise until doubled, about 45 to 55 minutes. Heat oven to 425°F. Make 3 parallel slashes on top of the loaf with a razor. Brush top with the egg white. Bake 10 minutes, spraying 3 times with water. Reduce heat to 375°F and bake 25 to 30 minutes longer. Cool completely on a rack. Makes 1 round loaf.

Provencal Cake

250 grams flour

4 eggs

200 grams green stoned olives or black olives

1 slice imported ham (around 1 cm thickness)

150 gram grated Gruyere or grated Parmesan cheese

1 soupspoon of baking powder

1 glass white wine

15 centiliters olive oil

Pepper and herbes de Provence and ground thyme (to
taste); no salt

Preheat oven to 350°F. Mix flour and eggs, then add olive
oil and wine. Add the olives and ham cut into small cubes.
Add cheese and baking powder. Put in a rectangular
cake mold covered with buttered aluminum foil. Bake
50 minutes, but cover the top of the cake after 20 to 30
minutes with aluminum foil.

Florence Penault

*This is perfect
for a picnic, with
an aperitif, or
for lunch with a
green salad with
only olive oil. Bon
Appetit!*

Joanne T. Stern

*This recipe
appeared in the
New York Times
magazine at least
30 years ago.*

Sour Cream Coffee Cake

1 cup butter

2 cups plus 4 tsp sugar

2 eggs

1 cup sour cream

1/2 tsp vanilla extract

2 cups flour

1 tsp baking powder

1/4 tsp salt

1 cup chopped and toasted pecans

1 tsp cinnamon

Preheat oven to 350°F. Cream butter and two cups of the sugar until very light and fluffy. Beat in eggs, one at a time, very well. Fold in cream and vanilla. Fold in the flour sifted with the baking powder and salt. Combine remaining sugar, pecans and cinnamon.

Place about one-third of the batter in a well-greased and floured bundt pan or nine-inch tube pan. Sprinkle with three-quarters of the pecan mixture. Spoon in remaining batter. Sprinkle with remaining pecans and bake about 60 minutes or until done. Cool on a rack. Serves 12.

David Alban

These are the pancakes I grew up with and are really the best. They are crepes, really, and great with a little orange zest in them.

Swedish Pancakes

1 1/2 cup flour

1 tsp salt

2 tsp sugar

3 well-beaten eggs

3 cups milk

3 tbsp melted butter

Sift flour, measure salt and sugar; sift again (optional.) To the beaten eggs add milk and melted butter. Pour into flour mixture and stir until combined. Pour half cup onto griddle to make large pancakes. Turn by folding in half with butter knife. Serve with fresh fruit, maple syrup or lemon curd.

Patricia
Ottens-Wainright

*In Memory of Doris
Corwin Ottens*

*Credits: Louise
Goller Corwin,
Guy Corwin, Reba
Corwin, Cathy
Corwin, Annette
Corwin, and Linda
Ottens Sauerteig.*

Weicke

BREAD:

2 diced potatoes

2 tsp salt

2 cups water

2 cups scalded milk

1 cup margarine

1 1/2 cups sugar

3 beaten eggs

2 packages of yeast placed in 1/4 cup warm water

10 cups flour

GLAZE:

1 beaten egg

3 tbsp sugar

Cook potatoes and salt in 2 cups of water, and then mash them in the water into a puree. Scald milk and then add margarine and sugar and mix well. Beat 3 eggs and add to the above mixture while partially warm. Mix yeast packages into warm water and then add to the above mixture. Add 3 cups of flour to the above mixture and mix well. Allow to stand in warm place until foam appears. Add 7 cups of flour and stir until it is tacky. Transfer to a breadboard that has been covered with 1 cup of flour. If necessary, use another cup of flour to handle the dough. Knead the dough 12 to15 times. Place this dough into a greased bowl and cover with a clean towel. Allow the dough to double in size. Grease a large cake or pie pan. From the enlarged dough ball, pull off cone-shaped "patties" (size of a small fist) and pinch the ends. Place 2 or 3 "patties" into the greased pan. Crisscross with the back of a knife over "patties" and then paint them with the glaze mixture.

Allow the loaves to double in size. Preheat oven to 350°F and bake 35 minutes or until golden brown. Remove from pans while hot. Slice and spread with butter.

Weicke is holiday potato bread that originated in Germany and came to Ohio in the mid-1800s. It was passed through many generations of the Goller/Corwin/Ottens family and into several states, and most recently to Chester, Connecticut. There is a tradition associated with the Weicke: the first blue-eyed boy who came to your home at the first of the year was given a Weicke; this visitor was considered good fortune. Our Grandfather had brown eyes and as a child was the first to rise in the morning before his blue-eyed younger brother. Eager for the potato bread on New Year Day mornings, he would waken his brother, and as a team they pursued their quest for a Weicke from a neighbor seeking good luck for the year.

MAIN DISHES

Kathy Morrell

Garlic mashed potatoes go great with this dish.

Apple Cider Pork

2 1/2 lbs boneless pork roast (or extra thick boneless pork chops)

1/2 tsp salt

1/4 tsp pepper

1 tbsp olive or vegetable oil

1 medium onion, sliced

1 cup vegetable broth

1/2 cup apple cider

1 tbsp brown sugar

1 tbsp cider vinegar

2 tbsp Dijon mustard

Spray a 12-inch skillet with cooking spray. Heat over medium-high heat. Sear pork in skillet 5 minutes, turning once until brown. Season with salt and pepper. Reduce heat to medium. Add oil and onions. Cook onions 12-14 minutes, stirring frequently until brown. Stir in broth, cider, brown sugar, vinegar, and mustard. Place pork in crock-pot. Pour cider mixture over pork. Cover and cook on low setting 8-9 hours or until meat is tender. Remove pork and onions and place on serving platter. Spoon some of the juices over pork.

Note: Gravy can be made with reserved juices. Pour juices into a 1-quart saucepan. Mix 2 tbsp cornstarch with 2 tbsp water and gradually stir into the juices. Heat to boiling over medium-high heat. Boil and stir 1 minute until thickened.

Beef Burgundy

Raffaela Cipriano

After cooking for 1 hour, you can also keep this at 225°F for 4 hours, to help reduce the liquid for a thicker sauce.

2 1/2 lbs beef tenderloin or boneless round steak

Vegetable cooking spray or olive oil

4 (+) cloves of garlic, minced

2 cups dry red wine (Merlot is good)

1 10 3/4-oz can cream of mushroom soup, undiluted

1 10 1/2-oz can beef consommé, undiluted

1 1-oz envelope onion recipe soup mix

6 cups sliced fresh mushrooms or soaked, dried Shitaki mushrooms

1 16-oz package frozen pearl onions

3 tbsp all-purpose flour

1/2 cup water

2 12-oz packages medium egg noodles, uncooked

1/4 cup grated Parmesan cheese

3/4 cup sour cream

Cut steak into 1-inch cubes. Coat an ovenproof Dutch oven with cooking spray; place over medium heat until hot. Add steak; cook 9 minutes or until steak is no longer pink. Drain well; set aside. Coat Dutch oven with cooking spray and place over medium heat. Add garlic, sauté 1 minute. Add wine and next 3 ingredients; stir well, bring to a boil. Return steak to Dutch oven; stir in mushrooms and onions. Remove from heat. Place flour in a small bowl. Gradually add water; blending with a wire whisk; add to steak mixture, stir well. Cover and bake at 350°F for 1-1/2 hours. Cook egg noodles according to package; drain well and place in a large serving bowl. Add Parmesan cheese and sour cream; toss gently to coat. Serve steak over noodles and with a good French baguette, alongside a glass of full-bodied, dry red wine. Serves 6 to 8.

Kathy Morrell

*This is one of
our family's
favorites—it
cooks up quickly
and tastes great!*

Beef Stroganoff

1/2 cup minced onion

1 clove garlic, minced

2 tbsp butter

1 lb ground beef

1 tbsp flour

1 tsp salt

1/4 tsp pepper

1 can (10.5 oz) beef consommé (not beef broth)

1 can (6 oz) tomato paste

1 tsp cider vinegar

1 cup (1/2 pint) sour cream

1 tbsp parsley

1 package egg noodles.

In large skillet brown onion and garlic in butter. Add beef, cook until browned, stirring to separate the meat. Sprinkle flour, salt and pepper over the meat. In a large measuring cup or bowl mix together consommé, tomato paste and cider vinegar. Pour over meat. Simmer uncovered 10 to 15 minutes. Blend in sour cream, heat through. (Do not overheat sour cream!) Sprinkle with parsley. Cook noodles according to package directions, drain. Serve meat mixture over noodles. Serve with rolls or hot bread.

Susan Daniel

I like to serve this with sautéed baby bok choy cut in half, tamarind sauce mixed in just before completion of cooking but still firm.

Braised Pork Tenderloin
WITH STAR ANISE, SWEET SOY, & BALSAMIC

1 1/2 lbs pork tenderloin, trimmed of any fat and silver skin

Salt and freshly ground back pepper

1 tbsp peanut or vegetable oil

3 large cloves garlic, crushed and chopped

4 slices peeled fresh ginger, each about the size of a quarter, diced

3 whole star anise

1/2 cup kecap manis* or <u>sweet</u> dark soy sauce
   *(Indonesian sauce, can be found at Asian groceries)

1/4 cup plus 1 tbsp light soy sauce

2 tbsp balsamic vinegar

1/2 cup water

1 to 2 limes, cut in wedges

Season pork with salt to taste, then season liberally with the black pepper. Heat a large skillet over high heat. When hot, add the oil and rotate the pan a bit to coat it evenly. When the oil is hot, add the tenderloin and brown it well, 3 to 5 minutes per side. Cover the pan and reduce the heat to low. Cook until the internal temperature reads 150 to 155°F on a meat thermometer, about 12 to 15 minutes. Transfer to a plate and cover loosely with aluminum foil. Let stand while preparing the sauce. Reheat the skillet over high heat and add the garlic, ginger, and star anise to the pan juices. Bring the mixture to a boil, stirring and scraping up the bits of garlic and ginger, until the mixture becomes fragrant and the juices are reduced by half, 1 1/2 to 2 minutes. Stir in the kecap manis, light soy, balsamic, and water and bring the mixture to a boil. Reduce the heat to maintain a low boil and cook, stirring occasionally, until the sauce begins to thicken, 5 to 8 minutes. Angle-cut the tenderloin into 1/4 inch medallions. Arrange the meat on a serving platter and spoon the sauce on top. Serve hot, with the lime wedges on the side. Serves 4.

Tina Von Flatern

Brie and Tomato Chutney Pizza

1 large pita bread (approx. 12 inches)

2 tbsp olive oil

1 tsp Basil Pesto

5-oz Brie, sliced thin with rind intact

4 tbsp Tomato Chutney (any brand, long as it has a little spice to it)

Place pita bread on lightly greased 12-inch pizza pan or 9"x13" baking sheet. Spread oil and pesto on pizza. Arrange Brie on pizza. Place small teaspoon-sized dollops of tomato chutney on Brie cheese. Bake at 350°F for approximately 8 minutes or until cheese melts and pizza is golden brown. Cool for 5 minutes and cut into wedges. Serves 4 as an appetizer or 2 as a dinner.

Cajun Salmon Pasta

Yvette Howard

This spicy pasta dish is one of my family's favorites.

1 lb boneless, skinless salmon filet

2 tsp minced garlic

4 tbsp butter

2 tbsp Creole Seasoning (McCormick®)

2/3 cup chopped green onions

1 12-oz can evaporated skim milk

1 lb thin spaghetti

4 tbsp chopped fresh parsley

Freshly grated Parmesan cheese

Cook and drain the spaghetti; set aside. In skillet, cook garlic in butter about 30 seconds on medium heat. Add the salmon and Creole Seasoning and cook, breaking up the salmon into bite-size pieces with a spatula. Add the green onions and continue to stir constantly until the salmon is barely cooked through, but not overdone. Add the evaporated milk, turn heat to high, and boil until slightly thickened. Remove from heat and add the cooked pasta and parsley. At this point it looks like there is too much liquid. Cover the skillet and let it sit for a few minutes, giving the pasta a chance to absorb some of the liquid. Toss again, and serve with freshly grated Parmesan cheese.

Dorothy Imagire

*This is like an
Iranian "frittata."
Though this green
(Sabzi) version
is traditional,
it is also made
with eggplant,
potato, cauliflower,
or almost any
vegetable. It must
be made with fresh
herbs to make it
really taste like
summer.*

Kuku-ye Sabzi

5 to 6 eggs

2 cloves garlic, minced

1 tsp baking powder

1 cup fresh cilantro, chopped

1/2 tsp cinnamon

1 cup fresh dill, chopped

1/2 tsp cardamom

1 cup scallions, thinly sliced

1/4 tsp cumin

1 cup parsley, chopped

1/4 tsp ground rose petals (optional)

1 tbsp flour

1 tsp salt

4 tbsp olive oil

1/4 tsp pepper

Chop fresh herbs with knife and cutting board. (A food processor makes mush of the flavors.) Break eggs into a bowl. Beat with fork. Add garlic, scallions, and chopped herbs. Mix well. Separately mix baking powder, spices, salt, pepper and flour. Then sprinkle on the eggs uniformly and mix in thoroughly. Heat 2 tbsp of the oil in 8-inch skillet on medium heat (an iron skillet is preferred). When oil is hot, add eggs and spread smooth. Reduce heat to low and cook about 12-15 minutes without stirring, until the bottom sets. When the bottom is browned (dark greenish) turn whole omelet over. Cut it into quarters to turn over, if too large. Add remaining 2 tbsp oil to the pan if it's too dry. Cook second side another 10 to 12 minutes. Remove from skillet, cut into wedge, and serve warm or cold. Cold leftovers are great in sandwiches.

Karen Kernan

Large Party Coq au Vin

2 lbs bacon, sliced crosswise into little squares

12 medium onions, chopped roughly

40 chicken thighs with skin and bones (don't use white meat—it gets stringy and flavorless when stewed this long, and use thighs with skin and bones for a thick, full-flavored broth)

32 oz button mushrooms, sliced in half (or quarters if they are very large)

12 cloves garlic, peeled and minced

1 cup parsley (chop half and save the rest for the next day's re-heating)

12 tbsp fresh tarragon (chop half and save the rest for next day)

4 bottles (yes, 4 bottles) dry white wine

Sauté the bacon to render the fat. Use a slotted spoon to transfer the bacon pieces to the casserole pot(s), and then pour the fat into a separate container. (You will use just as much bacon fat as is needed to sauté the rest of the ingredients. If you prefer, you can use olive oil for sautéing, with just enough bacon grease to flavor.) Brown all the chicken over medium-high heat. Don't crowd the pan, to ensure a nice brown crispness on all sides. Put all the browned chicken into the casserole. Reduce the heat to medium-low and sauté the sliced mushrooms, garlic, and half of the parsley and tarragon. This is quick—just a minute or so to coat and flavor everything before adding them to the casserole. Pour the wine over everything in the casserole pot(s) and bring to a boil. Reduce heat, cover loosely, and simmer for about an hour. Refrigerate overnight. To serve the following day, reheat gently and thoroughly on the stovetop or in the oven. Sprinkle on the rest of the tarragon and parsley. Serves 30.

Serving suggestion: If you happen to have a fireplace and a large cast-iron hanging pot, add a little theater to the evening by putting the warmed stew in the pot right before your guests arrive and serve from the fireplace.

This light version of chicken stew varies from the French classic by using white wine instead of red (and far less bacon fat). It is exceptionally tasty, simple, French comfort food. The recipe is very easy to do, even for inexperienced cooks. It's ideal for a large party because it should be made a day in advance. Just heat it up, slice some crusty bread, toss a salad, and enjoy your guests. You'll need a heavy skillet for sautéing and a two or three flameproof casserole pots (assuming you don't have a pot large enough for the entire recipe).

Linguini Puttanesca

Rosalie Rouillard

1 tbsp virgin olive oil

4 garlic cloves, minced

1 can (2 oz) anchovies, cut into pieces

1 can (32 oz) whole tomatoes

1 can (8 oz) black olives, chopped

2 tsp capers

1/2 tsp black pepper

1/4 tsp red pepper flakes

1 tbsp fresh parsley

1 tbsp fresh basil

1 lb linguini or thin spaghetti

Heat a large skillet, add oil, and when hot, sauté garlic and anchovies. Stir to break up anchovies. Add tomatoes and cook 10 minutes on medium-high heat, breaking up tomatoes with a spoon. Add remaining ingredients and cook 10 minutes longer. Cook pasta until al dente. Drain. Place in serving dish, pour sauce over. Serve with Parmesan cheese.

Kathy Morrell

This marinade is great on any kind of steak!

Marinated London Broil

2 to 3 lbs London broil

1/4 cup red wine vinegar

2 tbsp vegetable oil

2 tbsp soy sauce

2 tbsp ketchup

1/4 tsp onion or onion powder

1 tsp garlic

Black pepper to taste

Combine all of the ingredients in a large Ziploc bag. Marinate for 2 to 8 hours. Grill as desired. Slice on an angle.

Mary's Pesto

5 cups fresh washed and dried basil leaves

1 cup walnuts or pignoli (pine nuts)

9 cloves garlic, peeled and crushed

3/4 cup extra virgin olive oil

1 cup grated Parmesan cheese

Salt and pepper to taste

Place the basil, nuts, and garlic in a food processor. Drizzle in the olive oil as you process. Remove to a bowl and mix in the Parmesan cheese. Add salt and pepper to taste.

Doe Bartlett

Make in the summertime, when basil is in. This freezes well. It can taste salty because of the cheese, so it must be made to one's taste.

M. Jacobs

Improvised from a book by Paul Bowles.

Moroccan Chicken

1 to 1 1/2 lbs chicken breasts

1/4 cup strong olive oil

1/2 cup prunes, halved

1/2 cup sliced onions

1/4 cup cumin

1/3 to 1/2 cup chicken broth

Several shakes of cinnamon

Several shakes of ginger

Steep prunes in tepid water with cinnamon. Sauté onions in olive oil with ginger until soft. Remove onions from pan. Coat chicken breasts with cumin and brown on both sides. Add chicken broth, onions, and drained prunes to pan; cook over low heat for 20 minutes, turning pieces after 10 minutes. Thicken broth with a little cornstarch, if desired (add a small amount of broth to cornstarch, stir, and return to pan).

**Richard Messina
& Annie
Landfield**

*Exact proportions
of ingredients can
be created to your
own taste.*

Pasta with Zucca

2 to 3 cups Zucca (hard mellow Italian pumpkin), cut into
   1-inch or smaller cubes

1 head of garlic (or more), finely chopped

Olive oil

Salt to taste

Fresh ground black pepper

1 lb linguine

Chicken or vegetable stock, diluted with water as needed
   to provide liquid for cooking the pasta

Sauté garlic in a lot of olive oil, cover with lots of fresh
ground black pepper. Sauté squash until sharp corners
soften (squash is about 1/4-cooked through). Add stock
and liquid. Bring to a boil. Add linguine and cook al dente.
Remove pasta immediately and put into bowls (reserve
extra pasta, cover with soup and squash and grate lots of
Parmesan cheese).

Pernil

Bill Skrips

8 to 10 lbs pork shoulder

1/2 cup mustard

2 packets Sazon (Goya®)

3 tbsp Adobo (Goya®)

2 tbsp ground cumin

1/2 tbsp oregano

3 large cloves of fresh garlic, minced

4 tbsp Sour Orange (Goya®)

Mix all ingredients together. Take shoulder and peel back top section of skin. Rub all the seasoning into it. Poke holes all over the shoulder and stick seasoning into the holes, put skin back on, rub all over with seasoning, put in a plastic bag and marinate for 24 hours. Preheat oven to 500°F. Cook uncovered for 30 minutes. After this time, cover with foil and lower temperature to 325°F. Cook for 3 to 4 hours—check that it doesn't burn. After 3 to 4 hours, pinch with a knife; if the juices run clear, your Pernil is done. Once it's done, raise the temperature back up to 500°F for 10 to 15 minutes to crisp it—make sure it doesn't burn. Tap on it; once it's hard, it is done. Let stand for 15 minutes before cutting and serving.

Dave Duffner

Poor Man's Cassoulet

2 turkey legs

2 shoulder lamb chops

8 strips of bacon

1 lb small dried white beans

1 whole onion

1/2 cup olive oil

1 cup chopped carrots

1 cup chopped celery

2 cups chopped onion

1 cup dry white wine

1 18-oz can fire-roasted diced tomato

4 tbsp minced garlic

1 tbsp ground cloves

3 cups breadcrumbs

Salt, pepper, dried thyme, garlic powder to taste

This part may be done ahead—season and roast turkey legs at 325°F for 1 1/2 - 2 hours (rotate legs 2/3 way through roasting). Season and fry or broil lamb chops. Fry bacon. When cool, separate meat from turkey legs and lamb chops and chop meats and bacon into bite-sized pieces. Reserve meats. Place bones and skin in stockpot. Add quartered whole onion, seasonings and 3 quarts water (optional—pour off fat, deglaze frying and roasting pans and add to stock). Simmer for 1 hour. Cover beans with at least 2 inches of extra water. Soak beans overnight or bring to boil, then simmer for 1 ¼ hours. Sauté carrots in olive oil; after 2 minutes, add celery; after two minutes add onion. Season to taste, sauté for 6 minutes, stirring often. Drain and rinse beans. Combine beans, sautéed vegetables, meat stock. Bring to boil, simmer for 1 hour. Add meats, tomatoes, garlic, wine, and ground cloves. Adjust liquid level so that liquid is 1 inch above beans. Bake uncovered 1/2 hour in preheated 400°F oven. Liquid should be at level of beans. Taste and adjust seasoning. Cover with 1 1/2 cups breadcrumbs. Return to oven for 20 minutes. Fold breadcrumb crust into beans; recover with remaining breadcrumbs. Return to oven for 5 minutes. Serve immediately. Serves 8-10.

Hints for the lazy—Canned chicken, leftover leg of lamb, 5 cans of low sodium beef broth and 5 cans of beans may be substituted. Rinse salt syrup off beans, combine and cut simmer time to 1/2 hour. Also, carrots, celery, onions, garlic and olive oil may be combined and chopped in the food processor. Cut sauté time to 6 minutes. Vegetables will finish cooking as they simmer.

Pork with Turnips and Anchovies

Patty Langdon

1 tbsp olive oil

1 1/2 to 2 lbs boneless pork chunks (shoulder—butt or picnic—or chops from shoulder end of the loin)

Salt and pepper

2 tbsp minced garlic

2 oz (1 small can) anchovy fillets

About 1 1/2 lbs white turnips or rutabaga, peeled and cut in 1-inch chunks

2 cups chopped canned or fresh tomatoes, with their juices

Chopped parsley for garnish

Put oil in large deep nonstick skillet over medium high heat. A minute later, add pork and brown well on at least one side. Sprinkle with salt and pepper. Remove meat and turn heat off for a minute or so. Add garlic and anchovies with their oil. Cook over low heat, stirring occasionally, until garlic lightly browns and anchovies break up, about 5 minutes. Add turnips and raise heat to medium. Cook, stirring occasionally, until turnips begin to brown, about 5 minutes. Add tomatoes and their juice, then bring to a boil. Reduce to a simmer, then return pork to skillet. Cover. Cook gently until pork and turnips are tender, 30 minutes. If mixture is too watery, remove cover and raise heat to evaporate some liquid. Taste, add more salt and pepper if necessary, garnish and serve. Serves 4.

Lady McCrady

This is a Nicoise crepe. It is protein-rich and not fattening, and I think it is good for your muscles, especially in the summer. It is delicious with an arugula salad that has oranges chopped, red onion, cran-raisins, pecans, blue cheese and olive oil, or with fish or scallops or shrimp and a delicious sauce.

Riviera Club Socca Crepes

1 1/4 cup chick pea (garbanzo bean) flour

2 cups water

2 tbsp olive oil

Salt and pepper

Mix ingredients with a French whisk so it isn't lumpety. Some people like thicker socca and they use seafood or chicken stock, eggs and buttermilk, fennel seeds and a spot of baking soda. Either use a crepe maker appliance that you invert to get very thin crepes, or make the thicker crepes in an iron skillet with a little oil. Turn when the bubbles pop.

From the no-fuss
kitchen of Amy
Peters

*I love this recipe
because it can be
varied in so many
ways. As you'll
see, only a handful
of ingredients
are absolutely
required so this
pasta can be
whipped up when
the cupboard is
getting bare. Or,
add more flavors
for a more robust
dish. My family
has been making
this pasta for
years and we vary
the ingredients,
depending on the
time of year (lots
of basil when it's
growing fresh in
the garden, for
instance).*

Robust Pasta in a Flash

ESSENTIALS:

1 lb pasta, preferably small shells but any will do

1 package spinach, usually about eight oz. or so

Olive oil

Grated Parmesan cheese

NON-ESSENTIALS:

Minced garlic

Red pepper flakes

Chopped parsley, basil, oregano, chives, or other
   green herb

Capers

Chopped olives, black or green

Grated Romano or other cheese

As you are cooking pasta shells, choose the non-essentials you'll be using for this no-cook sauce. Put these ingredients into a bowl large enough to hold cooked pasta. For instance, if you choose minced garlic, red pepper flakes and capers, put these ingredients into bowl as you cook the pasta. If you love garlic, put in a several cloves' worth. The same is true for any of these ingredients. There is no one correct way in which to prepare this dish. Plan, though, to have a cup or so worth of ingredients in the bowl.

So, if you chop 3/4 cup olives, plan on a quarter cup or so of your other ingredients. Of course, for a more robust and savory pasta, more ingredients can be added. During the last 30 seconds or so of pasta cooking time, throw in the spinach—it will quickly cook. Drain it all in a strainer and toss in bowl with the non-essential ingredients, lots of olive oil and top with Parmesan cheese. Serve immediately. Want to keep it really simple? Simply boil pasta, add spinach during last 30 seconds, drain and toss with olive oil, topping with cheese. Even this simple combination makes a lovely quick meal.

**Terry Oakes
Bourret**

*When I was in
Santa Fe on a
painting trip I had
something similar
to this dish. When
I came home, I
tried to recreate
it. This is excellent
for brunch or
"brupper," and
goes well with
margaritas and
salsa music.*

Terry's Quesadillas

2 eggs, beaten with a whisk

1 tbsp water

1 tbsp butter

1/4 cup Monterey Jack cheese, shredded

Whole grain or flour tortilla, large

1 avocado, sliced 1/4-inch thick

Whole milk yogurt (Stoneyfield® – to be made into yogurt
    cheese – recipe below)

Salsa

Fresh cilantro

Make yogurt cheese: Fill cheesecloth with yogurt. Put into
strainer over bowl, and let the liquid drip out of the yogurt
for about 1 hour. This becomes a thick consistency like
sour cream, but much more flavorful and good for you.

In a frittata pan (a shallow side oval pan) or 8-inch frying
pan, melt butter slowly. Add eggs whisked with water and
cover the eggs with cheese and the tortilla. Make sure
the tortilla covers the egg. It might need to be tucked into
the pan. Cover the above with a lid and cook over very,
very low heat until the eggs are puffed. Check to see if it
is cooked under the tortilla by lifting up (it might be slightly
moist under the tortilla but should not be runny). Flip out
onto a warm plate. Places slices of avocado, a dollop of
yogurt cheese and salsa inside the omelet; fold over. Pour
more salsa and yogurt on top with fresh cilantro. Cut in
half to serve 2.

Leslie Ann
Powers

*This is good with
brown rice and
a green salad.
Leftovers can be
sliced and frozen
(I spoon a little
meat juice over
each slice before
wrapping for the
freezer).*

Turkey Meatloaf
NOT JUST ANY MEATLOAF!

1 1/2lbs lean ground turkey meat

1 tbsp parsley, chopped

1 small onion, finely chopped

1 clove garlic - finely chopped

1 tsp mixed herbs (I use Trader Joe's™ 21 Herbs)

1/4 cup ketchup

1 egg, whisked

2 tbsp goat cheese or other cheese - crumbled (optional)

1 box grape tomatoes - line up three in a row for each
slice

1 lb spinach (braised and squeezed, or buy frozen, cook,
and squeeze)

Take the first 6 ingredients and mix well in a bowl. Spread
half of the meat in a loaf pan, then layer the spinach,
tomatoes, and cheese. Top with the rest of the meat.
Bake in a 350°F oven for 30 minutes.

Uova in Purgatorio
EGGS IN PURGATORY – EGGS POACHED
IN TOMATO SAUCE

Sal Naclerio

*This was
my father's
favorite dish.*

1 small onion, chopped

2 to 3 tbsp olive oil

Pinch of hot red pepper flakes

2 1/2 cups crushed tomatoes

1/4 cup water

Salt to taste

4 to 6 eggs

Grated cheese

In a 9- or 10-inch skillet combine onion, olive oil and hot
pepper flakes and cook over medium heat until the onion
is lightly golden. Add crushed tomatoes and a pinch of salt.
Simmer for 10 minutes until the sauce has concentrated
a little. Break the eggs into the bubbling sauce. Cover and
simmer, cook until the eggs are done to taste, meaning
with fully set whites and runny yolks. Serve with grated
Parmigiano-Reggiano and a good crusty bread. Serves 2
or 3.

Zucchini and Noodles

Caren
Smith-Israel

1 box of tri-color pasta

3 to 4 zucchini, sliced

1 onion, diced

1 tbsp butter and olive oil

Salt and pepper to taste

3/4 of a 16-oz container of cottage cheese

4 tbsp shredded Parmesan cheese

Cook pasta per directions on box. Sauté onion in butter
and oil. Add zucchini and brown together. Add salt and
pepper. Drain pasta and put back in pot. Add onion and
zucchini to pasta. Add cottage cheese and Parmesan
cheese and mix. Serve immediately.

SIDES

Margaret Balian

Armenian Rice Pilaf

1 cup long grain rice

1/2 cup Vermicelli

3 tbsp butter

2 cups chicken broth

Salt to taste

Use a wide-bottom, heavy pan, with tight-fitting cover.
Melt the butter in pan, break up vermicelli in small pieces
and, stirring constantly, fry in butter until lightly browned.
Add the broth and salt. Heat and boil and then add
rice. Cover and cook over a very low flame about 15 to
20 minutes. Remove from flame and let rest for 5 to10
minutes. Stir once more before serving. Serves 4.

Braised Escarole

Raffaela Cipriano

*This recipe can
be doubled.*

4 tbsp extra virgin olive oil

1/2 cup thinly sliced white onion

1 medium head escarole, trimmed, washed, dried, and
   cut into 2-inch wide strips

1 tbsp chopped garlic

Salt and freshly ground black pepper to taste

1 tsp chopped fresh rosemary

1 tsp chopped fresh sage

1/2 tsp grated lemon zest

1/2 cup white wine

1 cup homemade or low salt canned chicken stock

1/4 cup grated Parmesan cheese

1/4 cup fresh breadcrumbs

Heat the oven to 325°F. In a 12-inch ovenproof sauté
pan, heat 2 tbsp of the oil over medium heat and cook
the onions until brown and slightly caramelized, 7 to 10
minutes. Add the remaining 2 tbsp oil, the escarole, garlic,
salt, and pepper and cook over medium heat to wilt
the escarole, about 5 minutes. Add the rosemary, sage,
lemon zest, wine, and stock. Bring to a boil and cook for
10 minutes to reduce the liquid. Cover with a piece of
waxed paper that lies flat on the vegetables and put in
the oven to cook until tender and a good bit of the liquid
is absorbed, about 40 minutes. Turn the oven to 400°F.
Remove the waxed paper, sprinkle the escarole with the
Parmesan and breadcrumbs, and bake until golden and
crisp, about 15 minutes longer.

Eggplant Towers

Susan Daniel

3 medium to large eggplants, each cut horizontally into
1/2-inch slices (slice so that each tower will have 3
eggplant slices)

26 ounces of your favorite prepared tomato sauce
(Portobello Mushroom by "Classico®" and Garlic-
Toasted Fennel by "Mario Batali®" work well)

1 lb grated mozzarella (part-skim works fine)

3 tbsp finely minced garlic

1/3 cup grated Parmesan cheese

1/3 cup finely minced *fresh* basil

Preheat oven to 400°F. Microwave eggplant slices
uncovered 7-8 minutes (depending on your oven) until
softened but not mushy. Cool. Layer eggplant towers
in a large glass Pyrex® dish beginning with the largest
slices. Each tower has 3 identical layers (quantities for
each ingredient are approximate): 2 tbsp sauce, 2 tbsp
mozzarella, 1 tsp garlic, 2 tbsp Parmesan, sprinkling of
basil. Repeat twice. Bake uncovered for 20 to 30 minutes
until cheese is golden brown. Serves 6.

Susan Guagliumi

*This freezes
beautifully, but
make sure it is
totally defrosted
before you bake.*

Lukschen Kugel

1 large package flat egg noodles

2 eggs

4 oz cream cheese*

4 oz cottage cheese*

1/2 pint sour cream*

1/8 tsp salt

Dash pepper

1/4 cup sugar

White raisins or drained canned pineapple (optional)

Preheat oven to 350°F. Boil and drain egg noodles. Add
a pat of butter. Add eggs, cream cheese, cottage cheese
and sour cream to the noodles, and mix well after each
addition. Add salt, pepper and sugar. Add raisins or
pineapple, if using. Put into a well-greased rectangular
casserole. Place a couple of pats of butter on top and then
sprinkle with chopped walnuts, cinnamon & sugar. Bake
for 1 hour.

*The more you use, the better it is!

Mom's Baked Beans

Mary Lou Fiore

*These are great
served with brown
bread.*

1 lb dried Great Northern® beans

3 tbsp green label Brer Rabbit® molasses

1 heaping scoop sugar

1 whole peeled onion

1/2 lb salt pork, rinsed and cut into 2- or 3-inch cubes

Salt and pepper to taste

Sort the beans and soak overnight. The next morning, boil the beans and simmer until soft but not mushy. In a large baking dish place the beans with the liquid (to cover by about 1 inch), molasses, sugar, onion, salt pork, salt and pepper. Mix well and bake in a slow oven (250°F) for 5 to 8 hours. Cover for a while and then remove the cover later, but do not dry out the beans.

Beverly Waters

Ratatouille

1/4 cup olive oil

1 eggplant (medium to large), chopped

1 onion (large), chopped

2 to 3 cloves garlic, finely chopped

2 (medium) zucchini, chopped

1 (large) green bell pepper, chopped

1 (28-oz) can tomato sauce

1 (28-oz) can crushed tomatoes

1 tbsp oregano

1 tbsp basil

2 bay leaves

1/8 tsp crushed red pepper

1 1/2 cup red wine

1/2 tsp salt

Water as needed

Sauté eggplant, onion, zucchini, and green pepper in oil until nearly tender. Add remaining ingredients and simmer on low for 1 1/2 to 2 hours. If more liquid is needed while simmering, just add small amounts of water. Serve over rice or noodles. Serves 6.

Susan Daniel

*Quick, easy,
delicious*

Sautéed Grape Tomatoes

2 tbsp olive oil

1 small shallot, minced

2 pints (4 cups) grape tomatoes

2 tbsp parsley, chopped.

Coarse salt and black pepper to taste

In a large skillet heat the olive oil over medium-low heat.
Cook the shallot stirring often, until softened, about 5
minutes. Add grape tomatoes and 1/2 cup water. Bring
to a simmer; cook covered 5 minutes. Uncover, and
raise heat to medium-high; cook, tossing often, until
tomatoes have softened and water has evaporated, about
3 minutes. Stir in chopped parsley. Season with coarse salt
and ground pepper and toss to combine. Serves 4.

Spinach Mushroom Gratin a la Teatro Piccolo

1 bunch spinach leaves, washed (3 times)

5 or 6 mushrooms, sliced

Pinch nutmeg

Ground pepper to taste

1/3 cup heavy cream

2 Granny Smith apples, peeled and sliced

Gruyere cheese, grated

Butter

Grease the bottom and sides of a gratin dish with the butter. Place an overlapping layer of sliced mushrooms in the bottom. Pour a small amount of cream over the mushrooms, enough to create some moisture and thus some steam. Sprinkle with nutmeg and ground pepper to taste. Pile on as many spinach leaves as you can manage over the mushrooms. The more the better, since they will reduce a great deal when they cook. Place a layer of apple slices over the spinach leaves. Build a final layer of grated Gruyere cheese over the apple slices, enough so that a thick layer of the cheese creates a cover for the apples, spinach and mushrooms, sealing the moisture inside. Bake in a hot oven, 425°F, for 15 minutes. Serve immediately.

Dita Carley

This is a knock-off of a dish that I had at a restaurant in Paris called the Teatro Piccolo, so the amounts are approximate.

DESSERTS

Jackie Knoll

Apple Coffee Cake

CAKE:

2 cups flour

2 tsp baking soda

2 tsp baking powder

1/2 tsp salt

1/2 cup butter, softened

1 cup flour

2 eggs, slightly beaten

1 tsp vanilla extract

1 cup sour cream

2 apples, finely chopped and coated in cinnamon and
sugar mixture

TOPPING:

1/2 cup nuts, chopped

1 tsp cinnamon

1 cup brown sugar

2 tbsp butter, softened

Grease a 13 x 9-inch Pyrex® baking dish. Preheat oven
to 350°F. Combine flour, baking soda, baking powder
and salt in a bowl; set aside. Cream butter and sugar. Add
eggs and vanilla and beat well. Add flour mixture and sour
cream alternately to creamed butter. Fold in apples and
then spread in prepared pan. Combine ingredients for
topping and sprinkle over batter. Bake at 350°F for 35 to
45 minutes until golden and apples are cooked.

Apple Torte

Pat Seekamp

CRUST:

1/2 cup butter

1/3 cup sugar

1/4 tsp vanilla

1 cup flour

FILLING AND TOPPING:

8 oz cream cheese

1/2 tsp vanilla

1/2 cup sugar

1 egg, beaten

4 cups sliced apples, peeled and cored

1/2 tsp cinnamon (optional)

1/3 cup sugar

Preheat oven to 450°F. Cream together the crust ingredients and spread on the bottom of a greased 9-inch Springform pan and 1/2 inch up the sides. Blend together the cream cheese, vanilla, 1/2 cup sugar, and egg until smooth and pour on top of the crust. Mix together the apples, cinnamon, if using, and 1/3 cup sugar and place over the cream mixture. Sprinkle with chopped nuts. Bake for 10 minutes, then lower heat to 400°F and bake 25 minutes longer until torte looks set. Serves 8.

"Artist Palette" Cookies

1/2 cup shortening

2 well-beaten eggs

2 1/2 cups sifted flour

1/4 tsp salt

1 cup sugar

1 tbsp milk

1/2 tsp baking powder

3/4 tsp nutmeg

1 package M&M® candies

Cream together shortening and sugar; beat well, until light and fluffy. Add eggs and milk; beat well. Add flour, baking powder, salt and nutmeg; mix well. Wrap cookie dough in waxed paper and chill. Roll out on a board lightly "floured" with confectioners sugar until dough is about 1/4 inch thick. Use a palette-shaped cutter if you have one or cut into the palette shape with a knife. Dip cutter in confectioners sugar each time. Place on a lightly greased baking sheet. Decorate each cookie with 3 or 4 M&M® candies to resemble paint. Bake in a moderate oven at 375°F for about 8 minutes, or until delicately browned.

Mary Lou Fiore

A good size cookie with a great taste, and a favorite with junior artists.

Bevi Bullwinkel

*This recipe came
from Key Biscayne
where we lived
forty years ago.*

Bevi's Key Lime Pie

Graham cracker crust (preferably your own made from
    box of graham cracker crumbs, sugar and butter—
    recipe will be on box)

2 or 3 eggs

1 15-oz can sweetened condensed milk

1/2 cup fresh lime juice (key limes if available)

2 tsp grated lime rind

1 /4 tsp salt

2 tbsp sugar (optional depending on sweetness of limes)

Beat egg yolks, milk, lime juice, rind and salt until smooth
and thickened (2 minutes). Beat egg whites separately until
stiff but not dry, adding sugar if desired. Fold into filling and
pour into crust. Set in 350°F oven for about 10 minutes
or until set or puffed slightly. Cool and add whipped
cream with additional grated lime or a thin slice of lemon
on top.

Anita Griffith and
Robert Parrott

*From Griffith and
Parrott Open
House.*

Biscotti Falconara Maritima
RAISIN ALMOND BISCOTTI

3/4 cup raisins

1/4 cup plus 2 tbsp Cointreau or Curacao

5 large eggs

2 1/4 cup sugar

1 tsp vanilla

1 1/2 cups blanched whole almonds, toasted lightly and
   chopped coarse

5 cups unbleached all-purpose flour

1 1/2 tsp baking soda

1/2 tsp salt

In a small bowl combine the raisins and the Cointreau
or Curacao, let raisins macerate for 20 minutes and
drain them well, reserving the liquor. In the bowl of an
electric mixer beat the yolks with 2 cups of the sugar until
the mixture is thick and pale, then beat in the reserved
liquor and the vanilla. In another bowl beat the whites
with cleaned beaters until they just hold stiff peaks, add
the remaining 1/4 cup sugar gradually, beating, and beat
the whites until they hold stiff peaks. Whisk one fourth of
the whites into the yolk mixture to lighten it, fold in the
remaining whites gently but thoroughly, and fold in the
raisins and the almonds.

In a bowl whisk together the flour, baking soda, and the
salt, fold the mixture into the egg mixture in 4 batches,
forming a dough, and divide the dough into fourths.
Working on 2 large buttered and floured baking sheets,
with floured hands form each piece of dough into a

flattish log 12 inches long and 3 inches wide. Arrange the logs at least 3 inches apart on the sheets. Bake the logs in a preheated 350°F oven for 20 minutes, or until they are pale golden, and let them cool on the baking sheets on racks for 10 minutes. On a cutting board, cut the logs crosswise on the diagonal into 3/4 inch thick slices, arrange the biscotti on the baking sheets, cut sides down, and bake then in the oven for 7 to 8 minutes on each side, or until they are pale golden. Transfer biscotti to racks to cool and store them in an airtight container. Makes about 60 biscotti.

Cecilia and Laurie

At least as good as blackberry pie, if not better, and so much healthier. The deal is you need to use frozen berries and they should thaw 15 minutes or so for the best "juicing."

Blackberries with Lime

As you sit down to dinner pour individual servings of frozen blackberries or Marionberries into glass dishes of choice. Top directly with brown sugar or honey to taste and quite a hefty squeeze of fresh lime juice. Leave out of the refrigerator, thawing, while dinner is served. Serve for dessert following dinner.

Alice Chittenden

Blueberry Cream Dessert

1 1/4 cup graham cracker crumbs

1/4 cup sugar

6 tbsp butter or margarine, melted

1/2 cup sugar

1 envelope unflavored gelatin

3/4 cup cold water

1 cup sour cream

1/2 tsp vanilla

1 8-oz carton blueberry yogurt

1/2 cup whipping cream

1 cup fresh or frozen blueberries

In a bowl, combine cracker crumbs, 1/4 cup sugar, and melted butter or margarine. Reserve 1/4 cup of the crumb mixture; press remaining crumbs in bottom of a 10 x 6 x 2-inch dish. In a saucepan, mix 1/2 cup sugar and gelatin; add the water. Heat and stir until gelatin and sugar dissolve. Combine sour cream and yogurt; gradually blend in gelatin mixture. Add vanilla. Chill until partially set. Whip cream to soft peaks; fold in yogurt mixture. Stir in blueberries. Turn into crust. Sprinkle reserved crumbs on top. Chill until set. Serves 8.

Blueberry Grunt

Chong and
Judi Lim

I quart blueberries

I lb French vanilla granola

1/2 cup honey

I stick butter

1/2 tsp cinnamon

1/2 tsp nutmeg

Heavily butter a 10 x 14-inch steel or glass baking pan.
Cut remaining butter into 1/2-inch pieces. Distribute
blueberries in pan. Drizzle with honey and sprinkle with
cinnamon and nutmeg. Cover blueberries with granola
and dot butter on top. Bake at 350°F until blueberries
begin to bubble. Serve warm with vanilla ice cream or
whipped cream, or both.

Joan Dulla

*My husband said
that this was
the best cake he
ever ate. I tried it
again and reduced
the oil (trying to
make it lower in
calories); it doesn't
work.*

Carrot Cake

CAKE:

1 1/2 cup salad oil

2 cups sugar

4 eggs

2 1/2 cups flour

2 tsp baking soda

1 tbsp cinnamon

1 tsp salt

3 cups peeled, grated carrots

1 8-oz can of crushed pineapple, drained

1 cup chopped pecans or walnuts

1/2 cup raisins

FROSTING:

8 oz cream cheese, softened

6 tbsp butter, softened

2 tbsp vanilla

2 tbsp grated orange rind

1 box (16 oz) powdered sugar

Combine oil and sugar. Add eggs, one at a time, beating
well after each addition. Sift together flour, baking soda,
cinnamon, and salt. Add dry ingredients to oil mixture,
stirring thoroughly. Add carrots and pineapple, fold in nuts.
Pour into well-greased cake pans. Bake 1 hour at 325°F.
Frost when cool. For frosting, beat cream cheese and
butter until creamy and fluffy. Add remaining ingredients.
Spread evenly onto cake.

Cherry and Almond Tart

Sheila
Kaczmarek

RICH SHORT CRUST PASTRY:

1/4 lb flour

1/2 tsp salt

2 1/2 oz butter

1 small egg or 1 large yolk

1 1/2 to 2 tbsp cold water

FILLING:

2 tbsp apricot jam

1/4 lb unsalted butter

1/4 lb fine sugar

2 eggs

Almond essence

1/2 lb ground almonds

1 lb 14 oz can of pitted red Morello (bitter) cherries
   (*griottes* in France)

Sift flour and salt into bowl. Cut up butter and crumble
into flour, mix in beaten egg and just enough cold water
to bind pastry together. Don't over handle. Wrap in plastic
and let cool in refrigerator. Preheat oven to 375°F. Line a
deep 9-inch flan case, buttered and floured, with pastry
(case should be at least 1 1/2" deep). Prick bottom lightly
and cover with coating of apricot jam. Beat sugar and
softened butter until creamy. Beat in eggs one at a time.
Don't worry if it separates. Add a few drops of almond
essence and ground almonds. Put in pastry crust. Drain
cherries, add on top of almond mixture. Bake in middle
of oven for 35 to 45 minutes until golden brown and
toothpick comes out clean. Serve warm with crème
fraiche or whipped cream. Serves 4 to 6.

Kathleen Dess

*This recipe
is adapted
from* Dessert
University:
More Than
300 Spectacular
Recipes and
Essential Lessons
from White
House Pastry
Chef Roland
Mesnier.

Chocolate-Dipped Almond and Hazelnut Biscotti

2 cups all-purpose flour

2/3 cup sugar

2 oz (about 1/2 cup) whole unblanched almonds, finely
   ground

2 oz (about 1/2 cup) whole unblanched nuts, finely
   ground

1 tsp baking powder

1/2 tsp baking soda

1 tsp ground cinnamon (or less, to taste)

3 oz (about 3/4 cup) whole unblanched almonds

3 oz (about 3/4 cup) whole unblanched hazelnuts

1/3 cup honey

1/3 cup water (in a 1-cup glass measuring cup)

Set a rack in the middle level of the oven and preheat to 350°F. In a large bowl, combine the flour, sugar, ground nuts, baking powder, baking soda, and cinnamon; stir well to mix. Stir in the whole nuts. Pour the honey into the water in the measuring cup; you will have 2/3 cup of the liquid. Stir the water and honey together, then add them to the bowl. Stir the ingredients together until they form a stiff dough. Scrape the dough onto a lightly floured work surface and divide it in half. Roll each half under the palms of your hands into a cylinder a little shorter than your baking sheet, making sure they are not too close to each other or to the sides of the pan. With the palm of your hand press down gently to flatten the logs. Bake the logs of dough for about 30 minutes, or until they are well risen and have also spread to about double in size. The logs are done when, pressed with a fingertip, they feel firm. Place the pan on a rack to cool the logs completely. Reset the racks in the upper and lower thirds of the oven but leave the temperature set at 350°F. Place each of the cooled logs on a cutting board and slice it diagonally every 1/3 inch. Arrange the biscotti on the prepared pans, cut side down. Bake the biscotti for about 15 or 20 minutes or until they are well toasted. Cool on the pan on a rack. Dip bottom third of biscotti into melted dark chocolate and stand up "chocolate base" on wax paper until chocolate is cool and hardened. Store the cooled biscotti between sheets of parchment or wax paper in a tin or plastic container with a tight-fitting cover.

Makes about 60 biscotti. You may substitute 1/2 cup of dried fruit, such as cranberries or apricots, for the whole nuts.

Chocolate Bread Pudding

Mary O'Connor

1 tbsp butter

2 1/4 cup half and half

1/3 cup brandy

3 cup semisweet chocolate chips

1/2 cup (packed) dark brown sugar

1 tsp cinnamon

4 large eggs

1 tsp vanilla extract

Pinch of salt

8 slices crustless country white bread, cut into 1/2-inch
    cubes (about 6 cups)

2 cups chilled whipping cream

2 tbsp sugar

Brush 8x8x2-inch glass baking dish with 1 tbsp melted
butter. Simmer half and half and brandy in large heavy
saucepan 3 minutes. Remove from heat. Add 1 cup
chocolate chips. Let stand 1 minute, then whisk until
chocolate is melted and mixture is smooth. Whisk in
brown sugar and 1/2 tsp cinnamon. Let stand until cool,
about 20 min. Whisk in eggs, then vanilla and salt. Stir
in bread. Let stand 30 minutes. Spread half of pudding
mixture in prepared dish. Sprinkle with 2 cups chocolate
chips. Cover with remaining pudding mixture. (Can be
made 1 day ahead of time; cover and chill). Preheat oven
to 350°F. Bake uncovered until puffed and firm in center,
about 45 minutes. Let cool about 10 minutes. Beat chilled
cream, sugar, 1/2 tsp cinnamon in bowl. Spoon pudding
into bowls, top with whipped cream. Serves 6.

Suzanne
Hens-Kaplan

Chocolate Truffle Cheesecake

18 Oreo® cookies, finely crushed

2 tbsp butter, melted

3 packages (8 oz) cream cheese (low fat is ok)

1 can (14 oz) sweetened condensed milk

2 tsp vanilla

12 oz (12 squares) Baker's® semi-sweet chocolate, melted

1/4 cup coffee-flavored liqueur (optional)

4 eggs

Preheat oven to 300°F. Mix crushed cookies and butter; press into a 9-inch springform pan. Beat cream cheese, sweetened condensed milk, and vanilla. Add melted chocolate and liqueur; mix well. Add eggs one at a time, mixing on low speed after each egg just until blended. Pour over crust. Bake one hour and 10 minutes or until center is almost set. Run knife around rim of pan to loosen cake. Cool before removing rim of pan. Refrigerate for at least 4 hours. Keep in refrigerator.

Cookie Bars

Lanette Barber

3 1/4 cups flour

1 1/2 tsp baking soda

1 rounded tsp salt

1 1/2 cups butter (3 sticks)

1 cup granulated sugar

1 cup packed dark brown sugar

2 tsp vanilla

3 eggs

1 1/2 cups semi sweet chocolate morsels

3/4 cup hazel nuts

3/4 cup pecans

3/4 cup raisins

In one bowl combine flour, baking soda, and salt; in another combine butter, sugars, and vanilla and mix until smooth and creamy. Add eggs to creamed mixture, one at a time, beating after each addition. Add flour mixture to the creamed mixture, a portion at a time. Add the chocolate morsels, hazel nuts, pecans, and raisins, one ingredient at a time, mixing after each addition. Baked in a greased 17 x 12-inch pan for about 45 minutes. Check after 30 minutes and watch carefully until done to your taste, soft or crunchy. Cut into desired sized pieces after cooling for approximately 30 minutes. Makes about 3 dozen large cookie bars.

Claudia Mathison

This dessert is so easy that I make it all summer long with whatever berries or fruit are in season. It's best served with fresh whipped cream, ice cream, or a fruit/berry sauce.

Fresh Fruit Cobbler

2/3 stick butter

1 egg

3/4 cup sugar

1 1/2 cup flour

2 tsp baking powder

1/2 tsp salt

1 cup milk

2 cups cut up fruit or ripe berries

Preheat oven to 425°F. Melt butter in a 9 by 12-inch baking dish (approximate size) or two smaller dishes. Mix egg, sugar, flour, baking powder, salt, and milk into a batter. Pour into the baking dish. Add fruit or berries. Bake for 40 to 45 minutes.

Timothy
McCann

Frosted Carrot Cake

CAKE:

1 lb (3 cups) carrots, finely grated

2 cups sugar

1 8-oz can crushed pineapple and juice

3/4 cup vegetable oil

1 tbsp vanilla extract

1/2 cup shredded coconut

1/2 cup unsweetened applesauce

4 large eggs

1/2 cup chopped walnuts

1/2 cup raisins

1 1/2 tbsp pumpkin pie spice

2 tsp baking soda

1 tsp salt

3 cups unsifted all purpose flour

FROSTING:

8 oz cream cheese, softened

3 tbsp butter, softened

1 1/2 cup confectioners sugar, add more later if necessary

1 1/2 tsp grated fresh orange peel

1 tbsp fresh orange juice

Preheat oven 350°F. Use angel food cake pan, bundt pan, 9x12 pan, 2 layer cake pans, or cupcake tins. Grease and flour pan or use cooking spray. Grate carrots. Beat sugar, pineapple and juice, oil, applesauce for 3 minutes. Beat in eggs one at a time, vanilla and carrots. Beat on High 1 minute. Put remaining cake ingredients into a bowl and mix with spoon. Gradually add remaining cake ingredients from bowl to batter, while beating on low. Beat 2 minutes, until well blended, scraping sides of bowl once or twice. Scrape all batter into pan(s). Bake 65 to 70+ minutes until toothpick comes out clean. Cool in pan(s) for 10 to 15 minutes on rack. Invert onto rack. Cool completely. Beat frosting ingredients on medium speed until blended. Frost cake. Refrigerate 1 hour before serving.

Betsy Chichester

*This recipe is from
my daughter Deb.*

Gingered Nectarine Cobbler

8 large nectarines, sliced

1 cup sugar

2 tsp cornstarch

4 tbsp lemon juice

4 tbsp crystallized ginger, finely chopped

3 cups all-purpose flour

3 tsp baking powder

1 tsp salt

1 cup cold unsalted butter

5 tbsp milk

3 tsp sugar

1/2 tsp cinnamon

Preheat oven to 400°F. Mix first five ingredients and pour into an 8 x 13-inch buttered baking dish. Cut butter into the flour, baking powder and salt. Add milk, then spoon over fruit. Mix sugar and cinnamon and sprinkle over the top. Bake 25 minutes.

Hot Milk "Sponge" Cake with Nutty Broiled Icing

Margot Levy

CAKE:

4 eggs

2 cups sugar

2 tsp vanilla

4 tbsp melted butter

1 cup boiling milk

2 cups sifted flour

2 tsp baking powder

ICING:

6 tbsp butter, softened

3/4 cup brown sugar

4 tbsp sour cream or rich cream

1/2 cup chopped nuts

1/2 cup flaked or shredded coconut

Preheat oven to 350°F. Grease and flour a 9 x 13-inch pan. Beat the eggs until light. Beat in sugar, vanilla, melted butter, and milk. Sift together and quickly beat in flour and baking powder. Bake 25 to 35 minutes. Mix together icing ingredients and spread evenly over surface of moderately cooled cake. Place under broiler until top starts to brown. Remove and cool.

Beverly Waters

Jewish Apple Cake

5 to 6 apples, peeled and sliced

3 tbsp cinnamon

5 tbsp sugar

3 cups flour

2 1/2 cups sugar

1 cup vegetable oil

4 eggs

1/2 tsp salt

1/4 cup orange juice

2 1/2 tsp vanilla

3 tsp baking powder

Prepare apples with cinnamon and sugar and let stand for about half an hour. Mix the cake ingredients—the batter will be extremely thick and heavy. Grease and flour a tube cake pan. Pour half of the batter into the pan; arrange half of the apples on batter. Pour remaining batter into pan, and finish with the remaining apples. Bake at 350°F for 1 3/4 hours to 2 hours.

Katie's Favorite Cake

David Frank

1 box yellow cake mix

4 eggs

3/4 cup oil

3/4 cup sherry

1 tsp nutmeg

Preheat oven to 350°F. Grease bunt pan with Crisco®.
Mix ingredients together and pour them into pan. Bake
until done, approximately 45 minutes. Flip out of pan and
dust with confectioner's sugar.

Lisa Billingsley

Lisa and Larry's Special Chocolate Cake
WITH CLASSIC BUTTERCREAM FROSTING

CAKE:

2 cups flour

1 3/4 cups sugar

1/2 cup cocoa

1 tbsp baking soda

2/3 cup oil

1 cup buttermilk

1 cup strong coffee

BUTTERCREAM FROSTING:

1 cup butter or margarine, softened

2 lbs powdered sugar

1 tbsp vanilla

Heavy cream

Cake: Sift together the flour, sugar, cocoa and baking soda. Add the oil and buttermilk. Stir until well blended. Bring the coffee to a boil and stir it gently into the batter. Mixture will be soupy. Bake in one greased and floured 9 x 13-inch pan or two 9-inch round cake pans for 35 to 40 minutes.

Frosting: Combine all ingredients in a large mixing bowl with a little heavy cream to begin. Slowly add more cream until spreading consistency is reached. Beat until creamy with electric mixer.

Matzoh Butter Crunch

4 to 6 unsalted matzoh boards

1 cup unsalted butter

1 cup firmly packed brown sugar

3/4 cup chocolate chips

Line cookie sheet with foil and place matzohs evenly
on the sheet in one layer. Combine butter and brown
sugar and cook over medium heat, stirring constantly
until mixture comes to a boil. It will be dark rich caramel.
Continue cooking and stirring for 3 minutes. Remove
from heat and pour over matzoh. Place in a preheated
350°F oven and bake for approximately 15 minutes
(check to make sure it doesn't burn). Remove and spread
chocolate morsels over hot caramel. Add nuts if desired.
Chill in refrigerator until set. Break into pieces and serve.

Jean Denholtz

*This is not only a
big hit at Passover,
but throughout
the year. You can
substitute saltines
for the matzoh if
you like.*

Kathleen Linta

This is one of my favorite recipes from my mother— the brownies are just irresistible!

Mom's Decadent Butterscotch Brownies

2 cups flour

2 tsp baking powder

1 1/2 tsp salt

1 package (12 oz) butterscotch bits

1/2 cup butter

2 cups firmly packed brown sugar

4 eggs

1 tsp vanilla

1 cup chopped walnuts

Preheat oven to 350°F and grease a 15 x 10 x 1-inch pan. Combine and set aside the flour, baking powder, and salt. Melt the butterscotch bits and butter in a double boiler. Once melted, remove from heat and stir in brown sugar. Cool mixture at room temperature for 5 minutes. Beat eggs and vanilla into butterscotch mix. Place in large mixing bowl. Add flour and walnuts. Spread evenly in the greased pan. Bake at 350°F for 30 minutes or until cake tester comes out clean. Cool; frost with icing made with soft butter, confectioner's sugar, milk, and a bit of maple syrup. Sprinkle top with chopped walnuts. Makes 35 2-inch squares.

Mudpies

4 oz unsweetened chocolate, chopped

12 oz bittersweet chocolate, chopped

1/4 cup (1/2 stick) unsalted butter

4 eggs

1 1/2 cup granulated sugar

1 tbsp brewed coffee

1 tbsp vanilla

1/2 cup cake flour

1 tsp baking powder

1/2 tsp salt

16 oz chocolate chips

1/2 cup walnuts

Preheat oven to 350°F. Grease a baking sheet or line with parchment paper. Combine unsweetened chocolate, bittersweet chocolate and butter in top pan of double boiler. When completely melted, continue to cook, adding eggs, sugar, coffee, and vanilla. Mix well until smooth. Remove from heat. Sift together flour, baking powder, and salt; gradually fold into wet mixture. Fold in chocolate chips and walnuts. Drop by large spoonfuls onto baking sheet. Bake for 15 to 20 minutes or until dough is firm and set to touch. Remove from sheet and cool on racks. Makes about 2 dozen large cookies.

Over-Night Cookies
MERINGUE AND CHOCOLATE CHIPS

2 egg whites

2/3 cup sugar

1 tsp vanilla

1 cup (1 small 6-oz package) chocolate chips

Food coloring (optional)

Preheat oven to 275°F. Use non-stick aluminum foil over
a cookie sheet (for easiest removal of cookies). Beat egg
whites until they peak. Add sugar gradually and beat until
mixture is shiny. Add vanilla. Gently fold in chocolate
chips by hand. Put about 1 tsp per cookie on cookie
sheet (cookies do not spread, so you can put them close
together). Put in oven and turn it down as low as you
can (125°F or so). Leave in over night or at least 6 hours.
Makes about 35 cookies.

Ellen Levine
Ebert

*These are easy
to make, since
you don't have to
bake them one
tray after the
other; they all
bake at one time.
Excellent for school
bake sales.*

Katrina Benneck

Whipped cream or vanilla ice cream make excellent accompaniments to this delicious cake.

Quick & Easy Apple Cake

1 stick unsalted butter, melted and cooled

2 large eggs

2/3 cups granulated sugar

1 tsp vanilla

1 cup flour

1 tsp baking powder

5 large apples (Macintosh or Cortland)

1/3 cup milk

Preheat oven to 350°F and place rack in middle of oven. Peel the apples and slice into thin slices. Add a bit of lemon juice and toss with the apples so that they don't discolor. Cream eggs and sugar until foamy. Add melted butter. Add flour and baking powder and mix together. Add sliced apples. Put the mixture into a regular-sized, buttered spring pan and bake on a center rack of the oven for about 40 to 45 minutes.

Ricotta Cookies

Julienne
Richardson

2 sticks butter, at room temperature

1 lb ricotta cheese

2 eggs

2 tsp vanilla

2 cups sugar

1 tsp salt

1 tsp baking soda

4 cups flour

LEMON FROSTING (optional):

1 cup sifted confectioners sugar

1 tsp finely shredded lemon peel

1 to 2 tsp milk

Mix butter, ricotta, eggs, and vanilla in one bowl; mix sugar, salt, baking powder, and flour in another. Combine wet and dry ingredients until the dough forms a large ball and all materials are well blended. Roll small dough balls about the size of a large marble and bake on an ungreased cookie sheet at 350°F for 13 minutes. If using frosting, mix together ingredients and drizzle on top of cookies.

Six Minute Chocolate Cake

Dita Carley

This recipe is from House and Garden *from 1976.*

CAKE:

1 1/2 cups unbleached white flour

1/3 cup unsweetened cocoa powder

1 tsp baking soda

1/2 tsp salt

1 cup sugar

1/2 cup vegetable oil

1 cup cold water

2 tsp vanilla extract

2 tbsp vinegar

GLAZE:

1/2 lb bittersweet chocolate

3/4 cup hot water, milk or half and half

1/2 tsp vanilla extract

Preheat oven to 375°F. Sift together flour, cocoa, baking soda, salt, and sugar into an ungreased 8-inch square or 9-inch round baking pan. In a 2-cup measuring cup, measure and mix together oil, water, and vanilla. Pour into the baking pan and mix with a fork or small whisk. When smooth, add vinegar and stir quickly. There will be pale swirls in the batter where the baking soda and vinegar are reacting. Stir just until the vinegar is evenly distributed throughout the batter. Bake for 25 to 30 minutes. Set the cake aside to cool, and if you choose to make the glaze, reset the oven to 300°F. For the glaze, melt chocolate in a small ovenproof bowl or heavy skillet in the oven for about 15 minutes. Stir the hot liquid and the vanilla into the chocolate until smooth. Spoon over cooled cake. Refrigerate for at least 30 minutes before serving.

Raffaela Cipriano

This recipe is from Recipe4Living.com.

Wolfgang Puck's Pineapple Macadamia Nut Upside-Down Cake

TOPPING:

3/4 cup shelled roasted macadamia nuts

3 tbsp unsalted butter

3/4 cup firmly packed light brown sugar

1 cup fresh cored pineapple chunks (5 or 6 slices), or 1 cup drained canned pineapple chunks

CAKE:

1/4 cup shelled roasted macadamia nuts

1 1/4 cups all-purpose flour

1 1/2 tsp baking powder

1/4 tsp salt

4 oz unsalted butter, at room temperature

1/2 cup granulated sugar

2 eggs, at room temperature

1 tsp pure vanilla extract

3/4 cup milk

Preheat the oven to 350°F. Spray a 9 1/2- or 10-inch round cake pan with cooking spray. First, prepare the topping. Put the 3/4 cup of macadamia nuts in a food processor with the stainless-steel blade. Pulse just a few times, until the nuts break up into coarse chunks. Set aside. Put the 3 tbsp butter in the cake pan and place over low heat just until the butter melts. Holding the pan with a potholder, swirl until the butter is evenly spread over the bottom. Sprinkle in the brown sugar and press it down in an even layer. Arrange the pineapple and chopped macadamia nuts in an even layer on top, breaking up the pineapple chunks if necessary. For the cake, put the 1/4 cup of macadamia nuts in the food processor. Pulse just until the nuts are finely ground. In a mixing bowl, sift together the flour, baking powder and salt three times. Add the ground nuts. Set aside. Put the room-temperature butter in another mixing bowl. With a handheld electric mixer on high speed, beat the butter until light and fluffy, about 1 minute. With a rubber spatula, scrape down the side of the bowl. Still beating at high speed, gradually sprinkle in the granulated sugar. Then beat in one egg at a time, scraping down the bowl after each addition. Beat in the vanilla. Reduce the speed to low. In three batches, slowly sprinkle in the dry ingredients, beating in a third of the milk after each addition. Continue beating until the batter is smooth. Pour and spread the batter evenly over the pineapple and nuts. Bake the cake in the preheated oven until a wooden toothpick inserted into its center comes out clean, 35 to 40 minutes. Remove the pan from the oven and leave it to cool on a wire rack for 5 to 10 minutes. Invert a serving plate over the top of the cake pan. Put oven mitts on both hands. Holding the plate and pan firmly together with your hands, turn the cake upside down. Lift off the pan. Dislodge and replace any bits of the topping stuck to the pan. Let the cake cool at least briefly before cutting it into wedges. Serve warm or at room temperature. Serves 10.

INDEX

CONTRIBUTORS